OLYMPIA

The Sound of the City Next Door

GrassRoutes Travel™

Other GrassRoutes Titles:
San Francisco: New View of the Barbary City
Oakland: The Soul of the City Next Door
Portland: New View of the Rosy City
GrassRoutes Kids **Bay Area**

Upcoming Titles:

Circle Guide Series
California Wine Country

BackRoutes Series
The Sierra Nevadas
The Cascades

GrassRoutes Kids
Oregon Coast and Valleys

New View Series
Seattle
Chicago
Vancouver

City Next Door Series
Baltimore
Detroit
Brooklyn

GrassRoutes Travel™

OLYMPIA

The Sound of the City Next Door

Serena Bartlett and Perrin Randlette
Illustrated by Daniel Ling

GrassRoutes Travel Press, Oakland 94609
Copyright © GrassRoutes Travel, Serena Bartlett, 2007
Illustrations © Daniel Ling, 2007
All rights reserved. Published 2007
LIBRARY OF CONGRESS CATALOGING-IN-PUBLICATION DATA

Bartlett, Serena.
   Olympia : the sound of the city next door / by Serena
Bartlett and Perrin Randlette ; illustrated by Daniel
Ling. -- 1st ed.
   p. cm.
   Includes index.
   LCCN 2007905818
   ISBN-13: 978-0-9791462-3-7
   ISBN-10: 0-9791462-3-2

   1. Olympia (Wash.)--Guidebooks. 2. Olympia (Wash.)--
Description and travel. 3. Ecotourism--Guidebooks.
   I. Randlette, Perrin. II. Title.

   F899.O5B37 2007   917.97'790444
                               QBI07-600225

Dedicated to

The hard working, conscientious, and fair practice farmers who bring healthy food to our tables

"Certainly, travel is more than the seeing of sights; it is a change that goes on, deep and permanent, in the ideas of living."

-Miriam Beard

Table of Contents

Acknowledgements
We'd both like to thank small, independent businesses, both owners and employees, and the artists that make our communities so rich. We'd also like to thank our talented contributors, Jesse Partridge, Kyle Tisdel, Ellen Dombrowski and Michael Robinson, our illustrator Daniel Ling, and our editors S. Edgar Paisley and Jeronimo Bay.

Serena would like to thank:
Writers and travelers before me, and the people who have listened to their inner voice to speak up in a world of contradictions. Thanks to my friends and family for their encouragement and support, spending time with me across this globe, laughing with me and always inspiring me to live out my dreams. Thanks to my incomparable and wise mother, my loving and encouraging Aunt Barbara, and talented and utopian father. Thanks to my teacher Khempo Yurmed Trinley Rinpoche.

Perrin would like to thank:
Thank you Olympia, for holding me safe through all the storms. Thank you Mom & Dad for raising me in Olympia and for raising me with Nature as our God. Thank you Aidan and Carson, who put-up with my mess and feed the cat when I'm away on adventures. Thank you Melissa for being my craft-hero and Paige for being so dang rad! Thank you Maize, your stories give me perspective. Thank you Grandma Mary, you showed me how to see the details of nature's beauty. Thank you Serena, for sharing your dreams with me. I am forever thankful for my mentor Barbara Bolender's teachings and guidance.

Introduction

The GrassRoutes Story

Like cracking open a dusty geode, travel has revealed to me the many facets of the world. The crystals I found brought me the clarity to compare my known world with that of the previously unexplored. I was able to connect truly with the rich diversity that abounds. No other activity has had quite the same impact, offering a unique experience where both commonalities and differences in the quilt of humanity were vibrantly displayed. Inspirations occurred while traveling around the globe and around the corner. The cities I have called home have given me plenty of refreshing surprises. Whether boarding a plane for another continent or walking a few blocks to a nearby neighborhood, no matter what my pocketbook dictated, I always managed to find new cultural gems.

As I walked the gangway on each return flight, I noticed that culture shock was as potent going home as when I had discovered new countries and traditions. Each time my reality was challenged with new ways of thinking and acting, I found I was less attached to one specific culture. After each journey I found I had new interests, different ways of dealing with difficult situations, and an altogether new perspective. The most important souvenir I brought home wasn't tangible—it was a more open mind.

As the pages of my passport filled up with stamps, I had a greater insight into each culture that could never have come from pictures or words. I also had plenty of stories to share. A minor bike accident I had in a Kyoto suburb brought a fleet of firemen to my rescue. A similar situation in Denmark roused little notice by other biking commuters but meant a gratis cup of black coffee as I waited for the city bike to be repaired. (Copenhagen is equipped with its own fleet of public bikes for anyone and everyone's use.) In London, a city stigmatized by many Americans as having the worst food, I have enjoyed some of the finest international cuisines. The more I traveled, the more stereotypes were turned on their head. In short, travel has taught me that no generalization really holds up.

I became a detective of sorts, unearthing cultures. Out of earshot from town squares or famous landmarks, I became familiar with local traditions. When I returned home I kept up the habit, discovering a wealth of intrigue in my own country. As a cultural tourist I discovered unique adventures right around the block. I have since made it my mission to seek out the non-traditional attractions and cities.

The people who hovered around the cathedrals and museums were of greater interest to me than the cold monuments. The living, breathing collection of foods and voices, footsteps on the roads and walkways—those were the things that attracted me. I witnessed the world around me blinking like a disco ball, with authenticity being overtaken by all things virtual, but I trusted another kind of travel. Wherever I was, the locals gave me the chance to have unique experiences rather than manufactured ones. By focusing on human interaction, serendipity soon replaced artificial stimulation.

GrassRoutes Travel was born out of my growing collection of ideas, inspirations, and frustrations. I remembered the grim fact that Americans (United Statesians, actually) have the fewest passports per capita. I made up my mind to promote world citizenship, but search as I might, I found no vehicle that expressed my ideas about travel. The Dalai Lama's wise words turned like a prayer wheel in my head: "If you have some [distress] you should examine whether there is anything you can do about it. If you can, there is no need to worry; if you cannot do anything, then there is also no need to worry." Doing something about it turned into GrassRoutes Travel.

The concept evolved from a bundle of notes collected on the road. Since I had never seen cities as separate boroughs, but as one entity, I didn't want my guides to divide chapters by neighborhoods. Most cities aren't so expansive that they warrant being divided by neighborhood. Also, chowing down on some messy barbecue didn't equate with a three star meal of braised rabbit, so I chose not to organize the guides simply by activity. I thought of the times I had woken up really early, the times I wanted to have a casual night out, or when I needed to get my creative juices flowing. GrassRoutes Travel had to be designed around these states of being: the mood of the traveler and the timing. To find a smash hit burrito at 1 a.m., just turn to the **Stay Up Late** chapter.

But organization wasn't the only thing I wanted to help evolve travel guides. GrassRoutes Travel is true to its name by including local businesses and their corresponding contributions to the greater good of the community. Restaurants that serve sustainably grown produce share the pages with shops that showcase works by local artists. Wildlife preserves are in the mix with co-operative bakeries and amusements that use energy saving techniques. Some of the best travel experiences I have had have been through meeting the locals in volunteer situations, so an entire chapter focuses on easy ways for visitors and residents alike to interact while giving back. Being conscientious about society and environment is a recipe for peace. Greet the world with an open mind: this is a message I hope to convey.

I was not born with a silver spoon in my mouth. Any voyage I dreamed of had to be financed by yours truly. What I found out was that travel could fit a limited budget. For a quick and cheap adventure, I could check out a new area of town or head to a museum on a free day. (I have included a **City for Free** chapter that lists some great money-less adventures). With a little perseverance, library time, and an inquisitive nature, I managed to find work exchange programs, scholarships, cheap fares, and home-stays. It was possible, even on my tight budget, to vacation on Mediterranean beaches for a weekend trip while living in Germany, explore the cobblestone walkways of Manchester, UK, and enter a floating temple on the Japanese island of Miyajima. There are ways to afford all kinds of travel. GrassRoutes is more than a guide to a city's attractions, it is a reaffirmation that authentic cultural experiences are not out of reach for anyone.

My first secret is printed right on the cover of this book: take a new view of travel. Try new cities, venture to places that aren't typical tourist destinations. Save time and money by choosing idyllic Rovinj, Croatia instead of over-priced and over-crowded Corfu, Greece for that above-mentioned Mediterranean vacançe. Not only are the next-door cities more affordable, but also they bring you closer to the region because they aren't built up as an attraction in and of themselves. Following the same example, in Rovinj, the native cuisine is delicious. Smoky, delicate fish straight from the surrounding waters with handmade lavender goat cheese just doesn't compare to the toast, eggs, and canned beans served at Corfu hostels to keep the many tourists "comfortable."

Along with the sights and sounds, local foods are a window into the uniqueness of each place. By focusing on culinary specialties, GrassRoutes encourages travelers to venture outside their comfort zone.

As you enjoy your travels, you can be satisfied knowing that you are a conscientious consumer. How is chocolate cake, conscientious, you ask? You bought it from an organic, co-operative local bakery that supports school gardening programs and purchases sustainably grown ingredients from nearby farms. When I found out how much fun, and, ok, indulgence, could be had while making a positive impact, I chose to be a conscientious consumer. The undeniable facts amassing about the current state of our planet necessitates that more of us make this choice. And with such a bounty of local businesses dedicated to this spirit of positive change, it is becoming easier to support such a philosophy. Each listing in GrassRoutes Travel meets these standards in one aspect or another. Whether re-circulating money into the local economy, supporting community outreach, protecting natural environments, or serving a healthy meal, there are many ways in which these listings participate positively. So while you are venturing out into the world and meeting real people in new places, your dollars are staying in the community, supporting everything from waste reduction to entrepreneurial youth, organic food to zero emissions public transit. Becoming a conscientious consumer gives each individual the power to effect positive change in the world.

I bring you GrassRoutes Travel Guides, created to benefit readers and communities. I hope you will try something new, even if you thought it was not possible. Having a genuine cultural escapade is directly proportional to your ability to let go of preconceived notions. All you need is an inquiring mind, a detective's spirit, and the desire to get acquainted with the world around you.

—Serena Bartlett

Our Criteria

Urban Eco-Travel is defined as businesses and activities that give back to their local communities through environmental, social or economic means. ALL businesses and activities must have local presence or be locally owned.

If you can answer yes to at least two of these questions, than the destination passes our test.

-Do they bank locally?
-Do they hire locals?
-Are they locally owned? (This must be a YES)
-Do they use energy efficient appliances?
-Do they sell fair-trade merchandise?
-Do they have a positive community benefit, i.e. bringing people together, providing community outreach and/or education?
-Are they careful where their ingredients come from? -Do they utilize fair trade, organic or locally grown products?
-Is their location environmentally sound, i.e. not on a landfill or the site or a chemical factory, not contributing to run-off, the building is made with green materials?
-Do they participate in re-use/ garbage reduction?
-Do they care about the environment, community and economy around them and prove it with their actions?
And last, but certainly not least:
-Do we love the place, does something make them special, do they blow our minds?

Using GrassRoutes Travel Guides

GrassRoutes Travel Guides employ a totally new system of organization that makes searching for activities, restaurants, and venues easy. This guide is organized by situation, with chapters like **Stay Up Late**, **Do Lunch**, and **Hang Out** that pay more attention to your state of being.

Organization by type of venue runs the risk of muddling a six-course meal with a drive-thru, just because both are technically restaurants. Instead, shouldn't guides be organized by what kind of dining experience you are looking for, rather than just that you are hungry?

Of course, there are those times when you are just looking for a restaurant or for a movie theater. It can be tough to kick that traditional categorizing, so we've got you covered in our Index. Here you will find destinations grouped by their respective category.

All phone numbers are in the **(360)** area code unless otherwise stated.

There is a price range key and also a "who to go with" key to highlight great spots to go with friends, family, solo, or for romance.

As authors we wanted to tell our experiences from our own perspectives, so we all used the 'I' perspective. The italicized initials after each review denote the primary voice (*sb*: Serena Bartlett, *pr*: Perrin Randlette, *dm*: Diana Morgan, *kt*: Kyle Tisdel, *ed*: Ellen Dombrowski, *jp*: Jesse Partridge, *mr*: Michael Robinson).

Price Key:

$- Cheap. Entrée prices are under 10 dollars.
$$- Moderate. Entrées between 10 and 15 dollars.
$$$- Pricey. Entrées are over 15 dollars, most are around 20.
CO- Cash Only, no plastic accepted here.

Company Key:

S- Solo. Places and activities that are great experienced alone.
Fr- Friends. Go with one buddy or a group of friends.
Ro- Romance. Great spots to go with that special somebody.
Fam- Family. Places for the whole family to enjoy.
PW- People Watching. Locations that are privy to an outpouring of interesting people. Slow down and take in the atmosphere.
Dg- Dog Friendly. Walk your pooch or settle down on the patio.

Service and Practicality Key:

WiFi- Wireless Internet available free of charge.
R- Reservations recommended
Vn- Vegan entrées available.
Veg- Vegetarian entrées available. If you see Vn, you can assume there is also vegetarian served.

Note: There are very few, if any Kosher or Halal restaurants and grocers, so please use Veg and Vn for pareve, or to follow your religious dietary guidelines.

Travel Tips

There are many different kinds of trips: seeing the seven wonders of the world, doing a trek or outdoor-focused voyage, going to a new city, traveling for family or business that may not involve choosing your own destination, rediscovering your own city when a friend comes to visit. For any given trip there are different ways to plan, but the core remains the same: stay open-minded. I like to remind myself that security is really a false pretense under which humans can never truly live. This is not to say that you should throw yourself to the mercy of the world. Safe travel is smart travel, but judgmental, pre-conceived notion travel can be just as dangerous. I will spare you with loads of examples, but suffice it to say, there is a lot out there, and your state of mind is directly related to how much of the world you will be a part of.

Here are a few tidbits on packing, getting around, trip planning, and safety that I have compiled over my years of world travel.

Trip Planning

My philosophy for trip planning could be considered a tad unorthodox, but let me just say, it has gotten me far. The bottom line is I don't over-plan. I pick dates that make sense and make the fewest reservations I can get away with. It is crucial to take into consideration factors of time, exhaustion, and exploration. Before embarking on a trip, I tell as many people as will listen where I am going and get their feedback and tips. I have the same talkative approach when I am there, meeting locals, and finding out their favorite spots. Look at books and magazines featuring the culture and history of the area before embarking on your trip, and keep a well-organized travel guide and a clear map with you while you're exploring.

Time Allotment

When picking dates, consider what kind of trip you want to have. One game plan is to spread out your time between different sights and get a good introduction to an area. Another is spending prolonged time in one or two cities, and getting beneath the skin.

In my experience, it is good to slow down the tempo of travel enough to smell the proverbial roses.

Reservations

There are a few practical reasons to make reservations, and there are also things to avoid planning too much in advance.

Be sure to reserve a hotel for at least the first night so you have somewhere to go when you get off the plane. Thumbs up to adventure, but even if you travel on a whim, I recommend starting on day two—after you get your bearings.

If your entire vacation will be spent in the same area, I suggest staying in the same, centrally located hotel the whole time, so you avoid carrying your stuff around. After all, you probably didn't travel to see different hotels, but to see the city itself!

In general, and this depends on the city and country, I wouldn't reserve many transit engagements. That way, if you want to extend your stay in a given spot, you can do that without too many trials and tribulations. Local transit arrangements are usually easy to book without much advance notice. Restaurants have widely varying reservation policies, so check ahead to see whether your dream meal requires them, or doesn't accept them. That way you can look around, act on a whim, and best of all, get the locals' advice. It is hard to get a good sense of a restaurant from its website.

Regarding hotels, make sure you are aware of each place's cancellation policy. Try to get an idea of the city first, before you book a room, so you can place yourself in the area of town that most interests you. (That is why **Lodge** is located toward the end of this book.) Be sure to reserve special event tickets and also tables at restaurants that require them. These are noted with an R in this book (see the key in **Using GrassRoutes Travel Guides**).

Packing

I like to have a good pair of pants that can match with different shirts. I bring one dressier outfit and a bathing suit. Bring more than enough underwear, but wear outfits that can keep their shape for two or three days of use, especially pants or skirts. You'll be meeting and interacting with new people everyday, so no one will know you wore the same outfit two days in a row. Buy extraneous items like sunscreen there. Remember, you will have to carry what you bring, so don't weigh yourself down. Check the climate and current weather conditions of your planned locations and pack accordingly. Try taking your luggage for a stroll in your own neighborhood before hitting the road. Then you'll know right away if you've over-packed, with enough time to do something about it.

Safety

All major cities around the world have some amount of crime. Please use your wits and stay safe. Try to avoid traveling alone to new places at night.

Other Tips

I always travel with the equipment that makes things less apt to bother me. On the plane I have earplugs and headphones, a sleep mask, a good book, and several bottles of water (provided liquid is allowed given new safety regulations). That way even if there is a screaming baby, my voyage will remain blissfully quiet. I find it is easier to make changes myself than ask others to tone it down. Get enough sleep before you fly. I recommend drinking lots of water the day before traveling and the day of—more if you tend to get dehydrated easily or are prone, like I am, to get headaches from the dry plane air. Boosting your dose of vitamin C won't hurt either.

Don't plan two activity-heavy days back to back. In general, it is good to have a combination of restful, educational, and physical experiences. That is one of the reasons for the GrassRoutes Guides organization. Traveling can include every type of adventure. Many other western countries allow for more vacation time than the United States, so Americans risk overdoing it when they actually get time off. Wherever you are from, make vacation time count by balancing your time and not trying to jam in too much activity. Ask yourself what you really want to see, and cut out the rest. Keep in mind that you can always come back, and be realistic about what you and your friends and family have the energy for.

I also recommend breaking into smaller groups when people have different ideas of what they want to see and do. Notations described in the **Key** indicate which restaurants are especially good for family, friends, going solo, and going for a touch of romance. Other activities include explanations that aid in trip planning to keep all members in your party entertained.

Contact Me!

The places and events listed in this guide are ones we thought were outstanding. Cities are constantly changing, so please contact me if you feel there is something we missed or if you find out-of-date information. Updates, new venues, and corrections will be posted on our website. We'd love to hear from you!

info@grassroutestravel.com   •   www.grassroutestravel.com

About Olympia

Budd Inlet

Brief History

For more than 500 years before white settlers came to the Puget Sound, coastal Native American tribes made it their home. It was an ideal gathering place for shellfish and salmon, and salt water beaches around the Olympic peninsula made natural spots for potlatches, where different tribes would come together to share the harvest bounty.

A closeness with the natural environment has been central to Olympia's growth and community since its very first inhabitants. Even Edmund Sylvester, the area's first "landowner" and founder of the city, came to the Sound so the salty sea would reinvigorate his ailing body. He and partner Levi Smith platted the town in 1850, changing the name from Cheet-woot, or place of the bear, to an silly amalgamation of their two names: Smithster. Other villagers got wise and started referring instead to their hometown as Smithfield until a newcomer to the town, Isaac N. Ebey, suggested the name Olympia in honor of the nearby range of snow-capped peaks, The Olympics.

In 1850, the town was a bustling new port, designed much like the tree-lined streets of the towns of Sylvester's native Maine towns, and was named the seat of Thurston County in 1852. By 1853 there were close to one thousand settlers, including one of the most active women's clubs on the West Coast, who which pushed for voting rights in Washington. A mix of Northeasterners, adventurous women, and Chinese made up the growing population, with their sites on economic success through logging or transit to various mines to the north and south. The attorney Daniel Bigelow perched his ornate frame-building house above the East Bay, which remains one of the oldest buildings of its kind in the state. In 1855, Isaac Stevens, the first territorial governor, designated Olympia as the capitol so that in 1890, when Washington achieved statehood, the bid of other cities to replace Olympia as capitol were denied because of the historical significance of the place. With a then modern streetcar line, street lamps, an efficient water system and a beautiful opera house and hotel in the midst of a luxurious natural setting, Olympia boasted the largest population in the Puget Sound until it was bypassed by the mainline railroad in the 1870's. From the turn of the century up until the 1960's, the lumber industry broke down the strong relationship between residents and their beautiful environment, with smokestacks reshaping the waterfront. The capitol building was completed just before World War II, and was luckily spared destruction by the infamous not one of the buildings devastated in the city-wide 1949 earthquake which devastated many city buildings. After the infamous storm on Columbus Day in 1962 when brutal winds of up to 78 miles per hour blew on, there seemed a transition in Olympia from industrial logging to education. Evergreen State College has since provided a cultural and community backdrop from which the town has once again bloomed as an environmentally-focused and naturally gorgeous place.

Each year, sustainably-caught shellfish fill the bellies of residents, and the salmon come up Budd Inlet through the ladder at 5th Avenue Bridge. Large leaf maples and Douglas Firs line the streets and extend into the plentiful green spaces reserved as park space by the government. The Yashiro-Olympia Bridge, celebrating Olympia's Japanese sister city, is muraled with mosaics that tell the story of the both communities and their strong bond with nature.

Olympia Now

As one of the founding members of the International Council for Local Environmental Initiatives, or ICLEI, Olympia has pioneered sustainability training and creative funding for pilot projects that incorporate sustainable practices into government policy and city life. Now there are some 650 towns, counties, and cities signed on, supporting each others' efforts to minimize global warming, including Oakland, CA, and Portland, OR, other GrassRoutes featured cities.

Although Olympia is so small that it can just barely be called a city, with its small size it has moved mountains and set a strong example for success in quality education, environmental policy, and awareness of the state of the Earth. Back in 1991, Olympia was one of the first cities to site global warming as a real and present threat and made strict policy that same year to increase green spaces and utilize renewable energy. The city's electricity is now 100 percent green, coming primarily from solar and wind sources. In short, Olympia is a place that has made living with the planet a daily mantra, without sacrificing economic concerns or cultural activities. If larger cities adopted the practices of Olympia, there would be a great positive the collective effect on the climate and on quality of life would be incredibly substantial and positive.

The social atmosphere of Olympia is rather laid back. Talking to strangers is common practice. You'll find that after just a few days in the Capitol City, you'll know business owners and locals by their first name, and you won't pass them by without a "hello." The relaxed atmosphere is contagious, so out-of-towners might have a hard time getting back into a rigid regime after spending time here. Somehow things get accomplished, and a small but thriving arts culture brings a great number of film, grafitti, theater, and, of course, music lovers together to showcase their works. Local painters and glass blowers are constantly inspired by the breathtaking environment.

The Farmers Market is open most days of the week, and is a hub where everyone in the town shops and convenes. There's something Old World about the capitol; in the summer it feels like you are on vacation whether it is your home base you are or not. The rainy season doesn't stop Olympians from being people are just as friendly and activities persist through any kind of rain. It feels like Olympia is still growing up, but its collective idealism has gotten it far. It is easy to wind around the downtown area without noticing the total lack of huge chain businesses, which have all congregated in other towns because Olympians wouldn't support their presence. Local business is so imbedded in the community that the last chain supermarket near downtown has been replaced by Olympia Co-op.

Though there is partiality to local business, businesses tend to close their doors quite frequently, as new ones crop up. My hypothesis for why businesses shift is that people are so friendly they give away too many samples or discounts. As a community, the common goal of preserving historic architecture has lead to a mix of structures remaining from different eras. From the beginning of Olympia to industrial remnants, it seems like everything that could be saved has been. An active bar scene is heightened by the college crowd and turns the otherwise placid downtown strip into an open-air party, especially in the warmer summer months. A gaggle of parks are cluttered with groups of friends whenever the sun is shining. It is a big kind of small town. A visit here will take the speed of life in the rest of the world down a notch; the relaxed vibe is infectious. As the saying goes, "it's the water." Locals say that if you drink from the natural springs here you'll be destined to return to Olympia. So come on over and see for yourself if its true.

Climate

Located on Budd Inlet at the southern end of Puget Sound, Olympia is home to a mild and humid climate, in fact it's among the top 10 most humid cities in the United States. Portland, OR has been nicknamed "Puddletown," yet Olympia trumps it in rainfall with an annual average of 50 inches. November is the wettest month with an average precipitation of 8.13 inches; still, you'll be glad you're not in Quillayute on the Olympic Peninsula, the rainiest place in the US. Summer temperatures tend to be in the 60's and reach an average maximum of 77° F in August. In the winter months the average minimum temperature is in the low 30's with January being the coldest month.

Geographically, Olympia is located at 47°2' North, 122°53' West and has a total land area of 18.5 square miles (43.3 kilometers square).

Neighborhoods

Downtown

Take in a breathtaking view of the Olympics, watch grey seals play among the sailboats, roam up from Percival Landing to Olympia's Farmers Market, and immerse yourself among vendors offering locally-grown veggies and addictive cinnamon roasted almonds at Jawa's Nut Stand. For a sample of the best coffee in Olympia, stop into B&B's tasting room, just up the street from the market. There are a handful of bookstores and quirky bars, antique stores and second hand clothing shops on Capitol Boulevard, so be sure to take home a tassel of local fashion.

Northwest

Buy snacks and refreshments at the Westside Co-op or go out for a meal at Vic's Pizza or Rosey's on Rogers. Walk down Garfield Nature Trail, one of Olympia's luscious gullies, to Budd Inlet. This close-knit area of town has some bigger shopping malls, great food and a supermarket-sized Goodwill store.

Northeast

Relax in the quiet of the Northeast neighborhood at San Francisco Street Bakery, and walk up to Bigelow Park, one of Olympia's oldest public parks. Brightly colored houses line the streets. The crowd is laidback and sociable.

South Capitol

Well-preserved homes from the early 1990's line the edges of Capitol Campus. Next door, the Washington State History Museum is housed in historic Lord Mansion. At the heart of the South Capitol neighborhood nobly stands Lincoln School, which is next to Stevens Field, where the neighborhood gathers for baseball games. Mysterious alleys, wrap-around porches, and gorgeous cottage gardens, all make Olympia's South Capitol neighborhood a great place to get lost on a long walk.

Smaller Neighborhoods

Olympia is a small capitol city, with big community feel. Even with its small size, the neighborhoods that would not be considered individual in other towns, in Olympia are tight communities close-knit units. People know their neighbors, and often organize regular get-togethers. These little enclaves of community don't have retail centers, but offer unique perspectives on the community life of in Olympia, and a tour of the its architectural diversity. I like finding locals-only spots to take long walks, and mix them up with the more impressive and well-tread routes like Olympia Pier or Priest Point Park. Take your time to explore the groupings of abodes and you'll be happily surprised to meet your neighbors du jour.

Here is a list of the smaller neighborhoods you might hear in conversation, or discover on a long walk between the larger communities: Goldcrest, Lakemoor, Burbank, Wildwood, Devon Place, Castlewood, Nottingham, Cain Road, Governor Stevens, Carlyon North, Holiday Hills, Briarwood, East Bay, Bigelow.

Maps

The following are maps of the major areas of Olympia to help you get around.

★ Look for GrassRoutes Travel Guides to these cities.

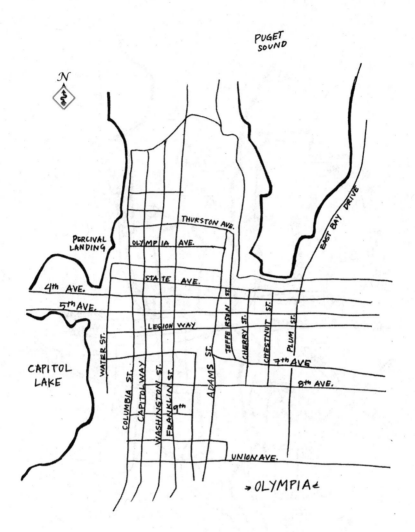

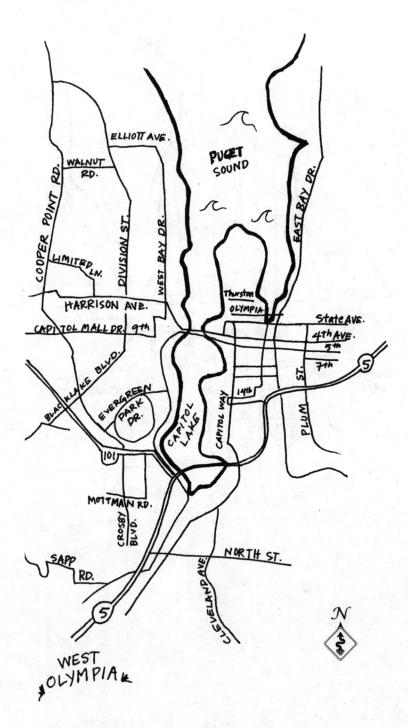

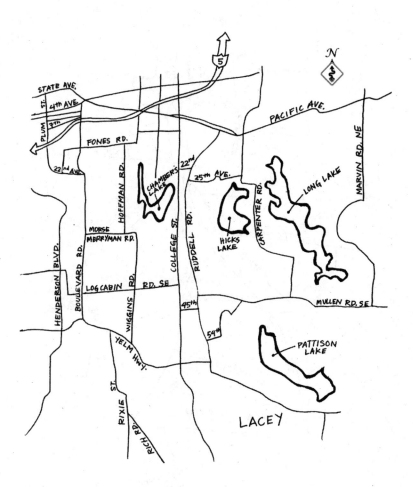

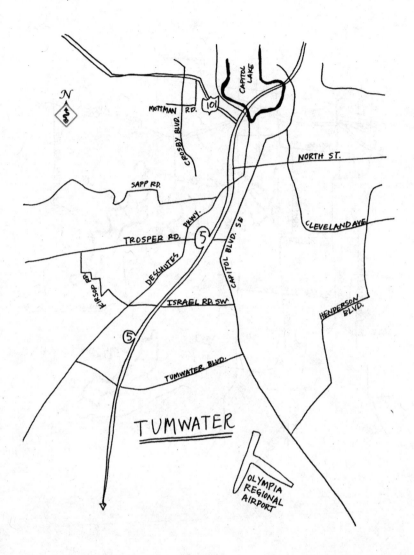

TUMWATER

Transit Information

Here are some options for travel that include everything from flying to walking. Even we conscientious travelers of the globe must at times make use of transportation options beyond walking! Weigh time, cost, and energy usage to determine which transport choice best suits your needs and the needs of the planet. There is something about the more time-consuming transit that provides a smoother transition to the next spot, though it may take a bit longer. Choose efficient routes to avoid wasting unnecessarily fuel.

Getting Here

Olympia is a friendly state capitol, where nature and community meet. The options below will set you on your way to what locals lovingly refer to as "Oly".

Amtrak
www.amtrak.com
Traveling by train is probably the least convenient but most scenic way of getting to and from Olympia. The Centennial Amtrak Station is located eight miles outside of town on the Yelm Highway; Intercity Transit operates hourly buses into town until 820p Monday through Saturday, 755p on Sundays. A Greyhound ticket is cheaper and drops you off right in the center of town, but there's something undeniably charming about taking the train. It's quieter, more peaceful, friendlier toward the environment, and the tracks north and south of Olympia run through lovely wilderness and back-country areas, with occasional views of The Olympics or Mt. Rainier.

SeaTac
www.portseattle.org/seatac
This modern airport is a hub of international travel with many direct flights to and from Japan, Taiwan and China. There's an underground tram that comes every two minutes, easily connecting the terminals. There are plenty of chain food options in each terminal, which are priced higher than usual, so I opt to bring a bagged lunch or recommend waiting until you are released from the security line to get some real grub. Although you cannot bring more than three ounces of liquid with you, and may even be stopped for gels like chapstick, you can still bring an empty water bottle that you can fill at a water fountain once inside, and avoid spending extreme amounts on bottled water. Security regulations seem to change with great frequency; check with the Federal Aviation Administration, www.faa.gov, to see what the current restrictions are regarding travel with gels and liquids, and determine if you can bring that bottle of water through security (you can usually fill it after you go through and before you board the plane). At the end of baggage claim there is a pleasant fountain with huge local rocks and a sculpture garden with historic planes flying from the glassy ceiling. It is a courteous aiport (if there is such a thing).

Capitol City Airporter Shuttle
www.capitolcityairporter.com
For a bit more than riding the bus to and from SeaTac, I highly recommend taking this shuttle. It is a carpool van that makes regular stops at hotels and hot spots from Olympia all the way to SeaTac, and north of that as well. If you like, you can pay a few extra dollars and arrange to have a door-to-door pick up. It is a much smoother ride, and even with the stops on the way, it takes far less time than the bus. At the far end of SeaTac baggage claim, you'll see the agent desk and out the sliding door of exit '00' sliding door the van will be awaiting you nearly every hour at five past. Take a glimpse of the historical planes and Northwest-style rock sculpture and fountain at the most done-up end of the airport, where the Airporter Shuttle gathers you.

Sound Transit
www.soundtransit.com

The bus system that runs to the airport and around the Sound is very inexpensive, but often requires a laid-back schedule and a sense of adventure. Times and routes vary, so leave ample room if you are planning to take the bus to a flight. Buses run later than shuttles, so for transit from SeaTac you'll be happy you have another option than trashing your bank account by grabbing a cab. The good news is that old buses are being replaced steadily with zero-emissions buses, so you can rest easy. Most buses run to and from Olympia Bus Station on 4th Avenue at Budd Inlet.

Cheap Airfares
Look around for an array of cheap tickets out of Sea-Tac from airlines like Southwest and Jet Blue. Regular cheap routes serve destinations like Denver, New York, Oakland (GrassRoutes hometown!) and more. Single direction tickets can get as low as $39 if you book at least two weeks in advance. Sometimes you can get two for one tickets on the bigger airlines like Alaska Airlines or United Airways. The websites that require you to purchase the tickets they come up with during a specific search are almost always less expensive than ones that enable open searches, so if you know when you are going, use these services.

Portland International Airport- PDX
www.flypdx.com

Portland is only two hours away from Olympia and there might be a good flight option that flies into the Portland International Airport. PDX is located just ten or fifteen minutes from Portland downtown where you can pick up the train or bus to Olympia in the Union Station area.

Greyhound Bus
107 7th Avenue SE at Capitol Way S
800.231.2222
357.5541, www.greyhound.com

Greyhound operates a number of departure and arrival times out of Olympia—call them up or check out the website for detailed schedules.

Shared Route

Across from the Olympia Transit Center
Franklin Avenue (Between State & Olympia Streets)
503.502.5750
www.sharedroute.org

Share Route runs their biodiesel bus from Portland to Seattle and back, passing through Olympia, on Fridays, Saturdays and Sundays. Fares are incredibly affordable—only $20 to get to Portland and $10 to Seattle. This is a much happier option than the Greyhound. Just look for the brightly colored bus.

Driving

Olympia is along the I-5 corridor that runs the length of the West Coast, so it is easily accessible to the road-tripper. There is always parking to be found downtown, so explorations are right at hand. You could also opt to loose the car and take the free Dash Bus around town.

Biodiesel Stations

Fast Fuels

505 Lilly Road SE, south of Martin Way E, north of I-5
943.1133

If you have a Fast Fuel card, you can fill up here, and applications are available on site.

Future Fuels, Inc

5347 75th Court SW, off of Greenridge Street SW
480.6452

Schedule a fill up and these guys will come to you to get your vehicle ready to be back on the road.

Ride-Share

www.craigslist.org

Craigslist is the online community board of much of the United States and the world. To search your local Craigslist, choose from the city list on the right hand side of the homepage. For the carless, or those seeking to be conscientious carpoolers, Craigslist has a special section under 'community' called 'rideshare.' Often people will post here who are looking for a ride or willing to accommodate passengers. Send a few emails back and forth and have a chat on the good ole telephone to make sure that you are comfortable with the person with whom you will be traveling.

A Note on Green Travel

OK, so buying carbon credits to displace your carbon footprint might not be the best long-term solution for reversing climate change, but while mentalities and technologies catch up, I am behind companies supporting green technologies where they cannot. Air travel is not great in terms of being carbon neutral, but many airlines are starting to spend money investing in energy efficiency to make up for their jet fuel emissions. When you book, pressure them to do so, or buy your own credits when you fly at www.carbonfund.org or another offsetting resource. The more customers ask about it while booking, the more they airlines will see it is an important step until planes can run on something cleaner. And just to compare, airplanes pale in the face of their friends the cruise ships, that take about six gallons of diesel fuel to move one inch. We at GrassRoutes do what ever we can to live with the Earth, but our work necessitates flying, so we try to use airlines that are more conscientious, and just go by the motto, "do the best you can." Perfection is not the goal, just be conscientious about your actions and you are sure to make a more positive contribution to the greater good. Weigh your options and... do the best you can.

Carbon Offsets

Despite the debates racketing back and forth about Carbon Offsets, it is an important stopgap measure that can really do a lot of good. Each carbon offset provider uses a calculator programmed to assume what a given trip will rack up in carbon dioxide emission. This mechanism considers factors like trip distance and the number of passengers on the plane, so if there are 100 people on your flight you'll only be responsible for your share. You then pay this provider to use your money to plant trees, or otherwise reduce carbon elsewhere. You aren't throwing your money away if you know where to get certified offsets, and thanks to the Center for Resource Solutions, there's a Green-E seal on offsetting providers who do the best job. Major air travel booking websites are helping out by making this a click option when you purchase your ticket. You can use offsets for your home's energy use, driving, or any event that results in carbon emissions. Look out for these companies that are doing a stellar job, and are thus endorsed by Environmental Defense (www.fightglobalwarming.com):

www.CarbonFund.org

www.atmosclear.org

www.Driving Green.com

Getting Around

Dash Bus

Dash

786.1881, www.intercitytransit.com

Dash is the free downtown transit option. Shuttles run down Capitol Way and around the Capitol Campus and arrive every 10-12 minutes, ending service in the evening. When the bus arrives, whatever your destination you'll have something to giggle about—Dash buses are postered with funny sayings like "Shopping for shoes? No time to lose!" This is not a late-night option with service ending as early as 5p on certain days. Free stuff is great!

Intercity Transit

786.1881, www.intercitytransit.com

Intercity Transit buses run all around Olympia, Tumwater and Lacey. The Olympia Transit Center is located at 222 State Avenue, where information can be obtained regarding all of the bus routes. Fare is $.75 for a single ride and $1.50 for a day pass.

Pierce Transit

800.562.8109, www.piercetransit.org

In cooperation with Intercity Transit, Pierce Transit, the statewide bus service, runs from Olympia to multiple destinations farther a-field, including Tacoma. Buses are boarded at the Olympia Transit Center, 222 State Avenue. A single fare is $2.

Flexcar
www.flexcar.com

If a car is simply a must-have for excursions to the city limits or beyond, Olympia has Flexcar. This is a national company with at least 10 other cities in their service area. Flexcar is a car share group that serves as an alternative to car ownership, business fleets and car rental. They do not claim to be a cheaper alternative to renting a car, but they claim convenience (usually there is a Flexcar to be picked up within a five minute walk from your current location), affordability (you pay by the hour, not by the day), lower age requirements (21 years of age and older), and sustainability (they sport hybrids and ultra-low emissions vehicles). Membership is required ($35 one time fee), and the application process can take up to one week, so planning ahead is required.

Resources

Stonewall Youth Center
705.2738, www.stonewallyouth.org

A non-profit organization, Olympia's Stonewall Youth offers weekly support group meetings, workshops, and fun events for queer and questioning youth up to 21 years old. They also hold an annual drag show, presenting community education in the funnest way possible and providing an opportunity for queer youth to be honored and seen. *pr*

South Sound Green Pages
www.olywa.net/speech

Each month a new edition of this free paper can be found scattered around conscientious shops and eateries in Olympia. Pick it up and you'll find out what is going on with local environments and snippets of what national and international incentives are being implemented to save the planet. Find out about great volunteer opportunities and resources for fun nature-oriented activities in the area. *sb*

KAOS Radio, 89.3 FM

www.kaosradio.org

Since 1971, the Olympia airwaves at the frequency of 89.3 mHz have been in the hands of KAOS, one of the country's most progressive and ground-breaking community radio stations. Although it's located on the campus of the Evergreen State College, KAOS is truly a community radio station in that anyone can receive free training in radio broadcasting and become a programmer. The station is almost entirely volunteer-operated and is well-known for its policy of requiring a minimum of 80% of the music played on the air to be independently produced. The programming itself is incredibly diverse. No matter who you are you're almost certain to find plenty of music on KAOS that you will like and quite a bit that you won't. There's also a good amount of public affairs programs to keep you up-to-date on progressive social and political issues ranging in scale from local to global. Check the programming guide; it's available online, or you can pick up a free copy from many local bookstores and other businesses. *jp*

FRO Radio, 98.5 FM

www.frolympia.org

Founded in 2001, partially as a reaction against perceived lack of commitment to social and political issues on the part of KAOS, Free Radio Olympia is an unlicensed pirate radio station broadcasting on 98.5 FM. In defiance of the heavy penalties (including prison time) imposed by the FCC for unlicensed broadcasting, FRO is on the air every day from 8p onward, broadcasting mostly radical and politically-charged music, spoken-word media, and left-wing news programs like Democracy Now. Professionalism is not one of the principles upon which the station is founded, and the programming is rough, uncensored, and often unstructured. However, tuning into Free Radio Olympia is often one of the first steps in getting involved in the town's spirited activist community, and it's certain to keep you well-informed about the latest political scam or cover-up. *jp*

Sitting Duck
www.thesittingduck.net
The free weekly paper of the South Sound can be found at just about every corner, in a stack by every community board, and on the tables of every coffee shop. Olympians rely on this helpful publication for up-to-date event information, most importantly of the musical variety. This city is full of great sounds, and there are shows almost every night of the week if you know where to go. Pick up a Sitting Duck and you'll be headed in the right direction. *sb*

Works In Progress
www.olywip.org
A progressive local free paper, WIP focuses in on activist concerns and reports in-depth on local issues as well as a scope of injustices farther a-field. It can be picked up at many local coffee shops, and is a great place to find current activist events and volunteer opportunities around town. Even if you don't consider yourself an activist, you'll be engaged by the strong writing. There's fun to be had at a beach clean-up day or at an environmentalist film screening you found out about inside WIP. *sb*

The Olympian
www.theolympian.com
The State Capitol has a premier newspaper that reports on local, national, and international affairs. Their website is fully updated; articles and topics are easily searchable. Papers are located at many stores, and are available at the coin bins on street corners. Major news stories are directly from The Associated Press. Local columns will give you a good sense of Olympians and their myriad activities. *sb*

Senior Services for South Sound
www.southsoundseniors.org
To find a hot lunch with perhaps the best conversation in town, the Senior Center is the jackpot. Regulars gather together and get into discussions in all topics, over inexpensive, home-cooked food. You must be a senior to attend regularly, but visits from people of all ages are welcomed. An online monthly activity calendar, a nutrition guideline program, their daily menus, and more helpful services for in-home care, or special needs can be found online. *sb*

Community Youth Services

711 State Avenue NE at Chestnut Street SE
943.0780, www.communityyouthservices.org

Community Youth Services is a one-stop for a myriad variety of services for at-risk teens and young adults. This non-profit provides career counseling, foster care services, a shelter, GED courses, family therapy, and diversion programs. There is also Rosie's Place, where youth under-21 can go to hang out, get their basic needs taken care of, and perhaps move into some of the other services that CYS offers. *dm*

Fern Haven Center

5721 Libby Road NE, south of 66th Avenue NE
754.1600, www.fernhavencenter.com

In an effort to help community members achieve harmony with one another and within themselves, Fern Haven offers counseling as well as workshops and retreats. The center focuses greatly on organizational dynamics, encouraging effective and respectful communication and conflict management. Fern Haven is influenced by the work being done at other retreat centers, such as Breitenbush in Oregon. *dm*

Sustainable Community Roundtable

209 4th Avenue East, Suite 206 at Washington Street SE
www.sustainsouthsound.org

Their motto is: "Sustainable development meets the needs of the present without compromising the ability of future generations to meet their own needs." Sustainable Community Roundtable exists to encourage living that echoes the guidelines of sustainable development. This organization provides indicators on community health and encouragement for businesses that take steps towards sustainability. Public forums and workshops provide a space for discussion about maintaining a sustainable community. *dm*

Olympia Lacey Tumwater Visitor & Convention Bureau
809 Legion Way SE at Plum Street SE
704.7544, www.visitolympia.com

The Visitor & Convention Bureau's very aesthetically-pleasing flash site has a slew of info on the Olympia area. There are links to lodging, dining, events and activities, as well as fun facts about the area and even information for people relocating to the vicinity. The website is a nice place to start for a quick orientation to the basics of the city. *dm*

Olympia Salvage
415 Olympia Avenue NE at Adams Street NE
705.1300, www.olympiasalvage.org
Open: W-Sat 9a-5p

There is a whole bunch lot of recycling that goes on in this society, which is great, but reusing is even better. Olympia Salvage dogma is: reuse, reuse, reuse. The non-profit provides deconstruction services to find a good home for the materials of your now-demolished garage. Their distribution center houses captured items from old buildings to be reincarnated in your next remodeling project. *dm*

OlyBlog
www.olyblog.net

Find out Olympia's latest news on OlyBlog. All contributors are "citizen journalists" who offer an alternative to corporate media. (They accept no advertisements or endorsements, only tips.) I like to browse the photos of Olympia's ever-evolving free graffiti wall. *pr*

Further Reading

To go deeper into a particular aspect of Olympian life, check out these other titles that are helpful resources for an insider's view. One of the great American authors, Tobias Wolff, wrote in great detail about the greater Puget Sound area, so his novels give a lyrical and historical picture of life in this part of the world. The beauty of the area has also been captured in some especially wonderful full-color photography books:

Olympia Tumwater and Lacey: A Pictoral History
by: Shana Stevenson, $29.95

12 Walks Around Olympia
by: Rosana Hart, $12 (look at Fireside Books)

The Highest Tide
by: Jim Lynch, $13.95

Kayaking the Inside Passage: A Paddling Guide from Olympia, WA to Muir Glacier, AL
by: Robert H. Miller, $18.95

Birds of Washington
Thayer Birding Software, $26.95 (look at Orca Books)

Thomas Brothers Guide Olympia
(detailed map book), $17.95

This Boy's Life
by: Tobias Wolff, $14.95

For International Visitors
Welcome— we hope you love Olympia a much as we do!

Required Documents
Before you plan to travel to the United States, contact your country's nearest U.S. Embassy or Consulate to determine the necessary documents required for travel to the U.S. You may be required to obtain a visa, passport or to pass certain health requirements, so allow enough time before your desired departure date to obtain this information. Visit **www.usa.gov** for more information for visitors to the U.S.

Customs
You must complete customs and immigrations formalities at your first point of arrival into the United States, whether or not it is your final destination. At this point you will speak with a customs officer and present your forms and documentation.

Travel Insurance
The U.S. has no compulsory government travel insurance plan. It is advisable to purchase private travel and health insurance.

Electricity
The standard electrical current in the U.S. is 110 volts. Most outlets accept two or three pronged plugs. Laptops and other electronic devices should be equipped with a power converter.

Currency
There are a number of large banks that will exchange your foreign currency to U.S. dollars. If you are arriving to the U.S. via an airport, most international airports have exchange bureaus located right at the airport. Travelex has two locations inside the Seattle-Tacoma Airport at which to exchange currency.

Washington Mutual
510 Plum Street SE # 101 at 5th Avenue SE
754.4288
Open: M-F 930a-530p, Sat 10a-4p

Bank of America
210 5th Avenue SW at 5th Avenue SW
753.8600
Open: M-Th 10a-5p, F 10a-6p

US Bank
402 Capitol Way S at 4th Avenue SW
753.9800
Open: M-Th 9a-5p, F 9a-6p, Sat 9a-1p

Emergencies

It is always a good idea to acquaint yourself with the emergency resources of an area you are visiting. Here is some important information in the case of an emergency:

Emergency Contact Information
9-1-1

Dial 9-1-1 on your phone only to stop a crime in progress, report a fire or call for an ambulance due to a pressing medical emergency. Like most cities, there are a limited number of emergencies that the 9-1-1 lines can attend to at a given time, so determine how urgent your situation is before making the call.

9-1-1 from Cell Phones

If you are dialing 9-1-1 from your cell phone, you will be connected to highway patrol and need to provide the dispatcher with details about the location of the emergency, your cell phone number, and, as always, the nature of the emergency. The location of cell phone calls cannot necessarily be determined like landline calls can, and sometimes calls can be cut off. If this is the case, call back. If you are in a moving vehicle, stop driving so as to not distance yourself from the location of the emergency. Check with your provider if there is a different emergency number you must dial from your phone.

Know Your Non-Number

Often incidences do not require the immediacy of a 9-1-1 call. For Olympia, the non-emergency number is 360.704.2740.

Emergency Updates

For updates on emergencies in the area, call the city line 360.753.4444 ext. 4011

City and State Emergency Departments

Here is the contact information for some important city and state emergency resources:

Olympia Fire Department
100 Eastside Street NE at 4th Avenue E
753.8348, www.olympiawa.gov/cityservices/fire/

Olympia Police Department
Main Police Facility
900 Plum Street SE at 8th Avenue
753.8300, www.olympiawa.gov/cityservices/police/

State of Washington Emergency Management Division
562.6108
www.emd.wa.gov

Office of Emergency Medical Services
236.2828
www.doh.wa.gov/hsqa/emstrauma/

Hospitals and Clinics:
Providence St. Peter Hospital
413 Lilly Road NE at Ensign Road NE
491.9480, www.providence.org/swsa/facilities/St_Peter_Hospital/
St. Peter's has emergency services. The emergency entrance is off
of Ensign Road.

Capital Medical Center
3900 Capital Mall Drive SW at Yauger Way SW
754.5858, www.capitalmedical.com
Emergency services available 24 hours a day.

Westside Westcare Clinic
3000 Limited Lane NW at Harrison Avenue NW
357.9392, www.westcareclinic.com
Open: M-F 8a–8p, Sat-Sun 9a–5p
This is a walk-in clinic. Appointments are not necessary.

Top Picks

San Francisco Street Bakery
For a croissant, coffee and conversation, there's nowhere we'd rather be.

Olympia Film Society
Hand-picked films both foreign and national grace the stage of our favorite pastime—the movies!

Capitol Lake
When you're here, you simply must lounge on the lawn and bask in quintessential Olympia.

Olympia Farmers' Market
Fruits, veggies and handmade jerky are elevated to a community adventure at the best Farmer's Market, where you can't help but run into someone you know.

Boston Harbor Pies
If you need a reason to visit Olympia, it is right here—cherry pie at this quaint spot—we can't get enough.

Lemongrass Thai
Both Thai and Vietnamese dishes are served with the perfect balance of spices at GrassRoutes top pick for meetings over grub.

Shipwreck Beads
This place is astonishing, we all love seeing this many beads in one place, no matter whether we have a project in mind or not!

Boston Harbor
The wildlife and splendor of Puget Sound wildlife is best seen from a kayak off this dock—we are all about it.

Olympia Calendar

Second Saturday Contra Dance
Every Month, second Saturday at 8p
South Bay Grange
3918 Sleater Kinney Road NE at South Bay Road NE
491.7033

Anyone looking for a good way to spend a Saturday night should look no farther than the Second Saturday Contra Dance held, logically, on the second Saturday of every month at the South Bay Grange, starting at 8p. There are often contra dances on the first and fourth Saturdays as well, though less often during the summer. People of all ages are welcome and it's not necessary to bring a partner; in fact even if you do you're both likely to end up dancing with plenty of other people over the course of the evening. If you've never contra-danced before then this is a splendid opportunity to learn how: every dance is preceded by a half-hour instruction session starting at 730p. The music is provided by various local ensembles, and is invariably superb; the opportunity to watch such spirited fiddle-playing is alone worth the $7 donation you'll be asked for at the door. But you're not likely to be given much opportunity to stand around gawking, and by the time the dance lets out around midnight you're almost certain to be gasping with exhaustion, dripping with sweat, and very satisfied indeed. The South Bay Grange is located at the corner of South Bay and Sleater-Kinney Roads, and you'll most likely need a car to get there. *jp*

Polar Bear Swim
January 1st at Capitol Lake

The morning after New Year's finds some 100 swimmers standing at Capitol Lake's edge, looking for their first thrill of the year. At four in the afternoon, after taunting Mother Nature by throwing a cooler full of ice cubes into the already-chilly lake, the polar bears rush into the water yelping and hollering above the cheering crowd. My friend Craig has been doing this for the past six years because, he says, "its fun and, I'll admit it, a bit crazy." This explains why the swimmer to crowd ratio is 1:4, there are more sane people in Olympia then insane. Or, perhaps there are just more wussies. *pr*

Ethnic Celebration
Beginning of February
Washington Center for Performing Arts
512 Washington Street SE
753.8585, www.washingtoncenter.org

Join up with residents of all backrounds, who come together during this time of year to share their cultures with each other through food, art, music, and craft work. Get in on the fun and get rid of the rainy day blues by learning Ikebana flower arranging while eating a Polish pizza: zapikanka. *sb*

International Fair Trade Day
May 12
Traditions Café, and other locations

Get in-the-know about the importance of buying fair trade and paying workers properly for their services. Even though serious issues are brought up here, it is a fun festival. with There are events ·for several days around surrounding the official International Fair Trade Day, including movie screenings, a community picnic, and talks with experts and supporters of this important movement. *sb*

Spring/Fall Arts Walk
Fourth Friday in April, First Friday in October
753-8380

Downtown Olympia is always a lively and active place, but never more so than during the bi-annual Arts Walk celebration. Taking place on the fourth Friday in April (the day before the Procession of the Species) and the first Friday in October, this festival embraces all artistic styles, including painting, photography, film, sculpture, poetry, dance, and, most especially, music. Sip wine and nibble on cheese while peering critically at the art on display in the Childhood's End Gallery or the lobby of the Olympia Hotel, or get all punked-out and blow out your eardrums at a free show at The Backstage or Manium. The streets become giant sidewalk-chalk murals, food-purveying establishments extend their hours to accommodate the evening crowds, and buskers assemble their audiences on 5th Avenue for juggling acts, magic tricks, and fire-blowing. Ducking in and out of shops, you'll find art in every nook and cranny: sitar music and fiddle tunes, open-mic poetry readings, and hands-on drumming workshops. Spring Arts Walk is unofficially carried over into Saturday as well, to give you something to do after The Procession (see below). Downtown businesses and the City Council love Arts Walk for the economic booster-shot it administers to the city center, but local punks and hipsters love it too for the opportunity it gives them to stay up all night playing music and drinking beer. *jp*

Capitol City Marathon
End of May
Starting at the Old Capitol Bulding

Each year the area's fittest competitors don their running shoes and start out on one of the most beautiful runs in the nation. Pass hilly trails along the Puget Sound, looking out over Mt. Rainer and the Cascade Range while you envision a smooth finish. Even if you don't want to participate, it is a weekend of fun for the non-runner in us as well. *sb*

Procession of the Species

April
Downtown
www.procession.org

This is the celebration of a community and its reverence for the natural world. It is the culminating exhibition after of collaboration between Olympians and their local businesses and schools. Come watch humans creatively disguised in animal-inspired costumes dance, shuffle, and flutter their way through the streets of Olympia. The community-centered, eco-conscious spirit of this town is nowhere better exemplified than at this joyful event. *ed*

Lacey Spring Fun Fair

Third weekend in May
St. Martin's University
5300 Pacific Avenue SE, Lacey
481.4393, www.laceyspringfunfair.com

This is the place to head if the kiddos are itching for my-size entertainment. For years the Lacey Spring Fun Fair has created a kids' world, entirely for the younger crowd, with crafting and games galore. For the older crew, there is a car show and plenty of food, music, and dancing. *sb*

Summer Volksmarch

First weekend in June
Northwest Trek Wildlife Park
11610 Trek Drive East, Eatonville
832.6117, www.nwtrek.org

Northwest Trek comprises over 700 acres and is home to a variety of animals from bison to otters to bald eagles. The Volksmarch, a non-competitive walk, is a great way to explore this park free-of-charge and catch a peek at some wildlife in their natural habitat. *dm*

Artist Studio Tours

Early June, 11a-5p
www.ci.olympia.wa.us/events
Various studio locations

Olympia artists open their studio doors to the public every June. See your favorite local artists at work and get the inside scoop about a wide variety of materials and techniques. Tickets can be purchased at The Olympia Center, 222 Columbia Street NW. *pr*

Duck Dash
First weekend in June
Tumwater Falls Park
www.laceyrotary.org

The Rotary club of Lacey dumps 14,000 rubber ducks into the Deschutes River and whichever duck crosses the finish line first wins their mommy or daddy ONE MILLION DOLLARS. Really. Sponsor a duck for five dollars, and your money will go to community programs. Munch on local foods while you see if your little yellow friend makes it through the chutes first. Even if it is fifth, you still get a Hawaiian vacation. This is a sight to see. *sb/pr*

New Market Pioneer Fair
First Saturday in June
American Heritage Campground
943.8778, www.tumwaterchamber.com

Every year a special class of eighth graders from Tumwater Middle School learn what it was like to live during 'pioneer' times, during the mid-1800's. The culmination is the New Market Pioneer Fair that showcases the lifestyles of these early settlers with hands-on activities for the whole family. *dm*

Swantown BoatSwap & Chowder Challenge
Second Saturday in June
Swantown Marina
1022 Marine Drive
528.8000, www.portolympia.com

The Swantown BoatSwap is an opportunity for boating enthusiasts to switch out last season's gear for new-to-you equipment and for chowda (as we like to say in Massachusetts) lovers to taste the Sound's best. This is a fun time for the whole family with live music and lots of food fixings. *dm*

Downtown Lemon Days
Second weekend in June
Downtown Olympia
753.8380, www.ci.olympia.wa.us

Every summer, the downtown commerce gets together a sidewalk sale of participating merchants. Even if you aren't in the mood to shop, I would recommend going for the free lemonade. *dm*

Super Saturday

Second Saturday of June, the day after commencement
The Evergreen State College
2700 Evergreen Parkway NW
867.6001, www.evergreen.edu

An Evergreen State College tradition, Super Saturday is a day-long festival of arts, crafts, music, food, and interactive fun for the whole family. With many community groups and cultures represented, sharing their passions or selling their wares, the festival draws thousands of people to the campus every year. Whether or not you're a kid, how fun is it to get your face painted?! *dm*

Annual Panorama Flower Show

Second weekend in June
1751 Circle Lane SE Lacey
456.0111, www.panoramacity.org

The residents of the retirement community at Panorama exhibit their horticultural prowess annually free of charge. Hundreds of plants will be on display, none for sale, but samples are given out, so stop on by. *dm*

Olympia Comics Festival

Late Spring
Various locations
www.olympiacomicsfestival.org

Meet the makers of your favorite cartoons as the inkers and liners are exposed at this annual show of cartoon art. Including a stage show, signings at Danger Room in downtown Olympia, and a chance to ham-it-up with the guests of honor: professionals that are in the spotlight. The Comic Fest is also a great chance to show off your own strip. *sb*

Blintzapolooza

201 8th Avenue SE
754.8519

An atypical, yet ideal combination event at Temple Beth Hatfiloh including a used book sale with bagels and blintzes in the kitchen. Stuff your face with these classic creamy folded crêpes and stack books with your other hand. All proceeds go to local community organizations like SafePlace and the Refugee Center. *pr*

Capitol Lakefair Car Show
Third Friday in June
Marathon Park, off Deschutes Parkway
www.lakefair.org
Admission: $20/vehicle, free without vehicle

A chance for car enthusiasts to strut their stuff and take a peek at other hot rods and custom rides, the Capitol Lakefair Car Show sets up shop on the south side of the lake in Marathon Park. If you have a special auto to display, the first 50 to register get to participate in the "Cruise-In" that kicks-off the festivities, so sign up early. *dm*

Olympia Air Show
Third weekend in June
Olympic Flight Museum
7637-A Old Highway 99 SE
705.3925, www.olympicflightmuseum.com
Admission: $10 CO

We can swim, we can run, but we can't fly. I think that humans will always suffer from bird envy. Luckily, we compensate for our physical limitations with those sometimes ridiculous mechanisms that we invent in order to achieve those seemingly impossible dreams. Planes allow us to soar with the best of nature's aviators and the Olympia Air Show is a display of historical and contemporary crafts alike—for the finale show there is aerobatic flying. *dm*

Capital City Pride Weekend
Third weekend in June
Various Locations
www.capitalcitypride.net

Drag shows, gay chorus performances, kids activities, and a parade make this weekend two full days of pride and celebration. City residents from all parts of the rainbow spectrum take part in the festivities at this annual event. *dm*

Dixieland Jazz Festival

Last Weekend in June
Multiple Venues
943.9123
Admission: $7, daily passes available also

A kick of New Orleans in the Northwest, the Dixieland Jazz Festival is a weekend of blowing brasses and boogie beats. Tickets don't come cheap, but may be worth it to catch some historically significant music and just to enjoy the bopping sounds of Dixieland. *dm*

Downtown Neighborhood Association's Street Fair

End of June
www.olydna.com
5th Avenue, Downtown Olympia

Olympia's do-it-yourself street fair is run by the vendors themselves, who volunteer their time to put on this sweet city market where everyone is welcome to sell their wares. Tables and clothing racks line 5th Avenue between Capitol and Washington Streets. I enjoy milling around, picking through the contents of everyone's closets and garages. The axiom "one man's junk is another man's treasure" holds true at DNA's Street Fair. I've always found at least one major score. *pr*

What You Got! Film Festival

Early July
Olympia Free School
Various Locations

The youth of Olympia get together every year at Olympia Free School to show off their films and their music. Take a workshop or volunteer to help out make the wheels run smoothly at this event. Get a real sense of what the younger generation is thinking about and how they are dealing with the current state of affairs with a night of watching films. The whole community comes together for this one. *sb*

Wildlife Festival

Middle of July
3111 Offut Lake Road, Tenino
264.4495, www.wolfhaven.org

Tour the Wolf Haven sancutary for a reduced rate armed with new knowledge of the wildlife that abounds in this area of the world. This is a weekend long of wolves, campfires, arts and crafts, organic food, and swing dancing. Get into the spirit! *sb*

Lakefair Run

Third Saturday in July
Capitol Lake
705.2508, www.ontherunevents.com/lakfair

Held annually, the Lakefair Run is both a 8k and 3k road race/walk for the active people and visitors of Olympia. The course travels on Deschutes Parkway, by Capitol Lake, and has been going on for over 30 years. *dm*

Garden Rhapsodies Tour

Last weekend in June
Ask for info at the Olympia Farmers' Market Garden booth

Once a year the master gardeners of Olympia pair up with the Native Plant Salvage Project and select eight or so gardens to host their garden tour. It's an opportunity to snoop around the beautiful and distinctive gardens. I enjoy just driving by wondering how gardens get so lovely! The owners and volunteers are standing by ready to answer questions about gardening techniques and native planets, and they have a shuttle bus from garden to garden. *pr*

Pet Parade

Middle of August
Capitol Lake Park, Downtown Olympia
786.5441

It is fun to see how owners can so closely match their pets. Or is it that the pets match their owners? Regardless, Olympia's Pet Parade is a wonderful opportunity to witness the love and celebrate the connections between humans and their four-legged loves. *pr*

Music in the Park
Sylvester Park Capitol Way and Legion Way
Summertime in Olympia means music in the park every Wednesday, July through August. The Olympia Downtown Association hosts open-air concerts showcasing local jazz, bluegrass, rock, and blues. Sylvester Park happily overflows with picnic blankets and kids dancing into the night. *pr*

Olympia Hemp Festival at Heritage Park
Last weekend in August
Sa 11a-12a, Su 11a-8p
www.olyhempfest.com
The Olympia Hemp Fest is a celebration of conscious living. In the heat of August, 500 plus people meet to share music, information, and activities. In between speakers, taste the newest hemp foods, along with organic and vegan options. *pr*

Olympia Experimental Music Festival
Eagles Hall
805 4th Avenue E at Plum Street SE
Third week in June
A wide array of sounds performed by masters of innovation, the Olympia Experimental Music Festival hosts experimental performers from around the world, bringing the sound-freaks out of their basement recording studios and into the spotlight. *pr*

Olympic Music Festival
June through September, Sa-Su 2-6p
7360 Center Road, Quilcene
206.527.8839, www.olympicmusicfestival.org
The Olympic Peninsula is a wondrous place to explore, and combining these sights with the sounds of chamber music is a dream come true. Bring a picnic and some sunscreen and get your ears ready for some beautiful melodies. *sb*

Sand in the City
Last weekend in August
Port Plaza
701 Columbia Street NW
www.hocm.org/sitc/html/about.html
A benefit for Hands On Children's Museum, Sand in the City combines art with play. Local businesses sponsor teams of sand artists to build sand-sculptures. We are talking some pretty impressive sand-sculptures: mermaids with flowers in their hair and sports cars on a raceway. *pr*

Percival Play Day
Third weekend in September
Percival Landing Park
570.5858, www.ci.olympia.wa.us
Another way to get the family out and about is Percival Play Day. City vehicles are on display to be explored and there is, of course, the requisite crafting, eating, and general playful vibe of a festival. *dm*

Harvest Festival
First Weekend in October
602 Deschutes Way SW, Tumwater
754.4163
Located in Tumwater, just up the road from Tumwater Walls Park, the Henderson House Museum hosts a harvest festival every autumn. In honor of the returning the salmon there is celebratation with snacks, games, and fresh-pressed cider, complete with children dressed as little pioneers. Bundle up and go celebrate welcome the harvest. *pr*

Olympia Film Festival
Early November
206 5th Avenue SE at Washington Street SE
754.5378, www.olympiafilmfestival.org

The Olympia Film Society's annual film festival has taken place in early November every year since 1984, and many lives come to a complete halt during these ten days—devoted entirely to independent film. Even if you take a leave of absence from your job and neglect your friends and loved ones, you'll still find it impossible to take in the many overlapping events this massive festival has to offer, so obtain a free copy of the schedule and plan your time carefully. Many noteworthy foreign and independent films have had their premier here, and many forgotten gems are resurrected and given new life on the Capital Theater's screen. In addition to feature-length films, the Olympia Film Festival includes shorts, guest lectures, musical events, and parties, overflowing the bounds of the Capitol Theater into many surrounding businesses and venues. The film festival closes every year with All Freakin' Night, your opportunity to test your endurance with horror movies until dawn: definitely not an event for the overly mature. Entry into individual films is $5 for OFS members, $8 for non-members, and an entire festival pass costs $75. *pr*

Up Early

Early bird specials and morning treats

Rosey's on Rogers

It is much easier to get up and get out knowing there are fantastic omelets, crêpes and all manner of breakfast fare at the end of the proverbial rainbow. Whether you have to be dragged from your bed, or are the one with that annoying extra morning gusto, follow your nose on a whim and enjoy the early hours of the day. Start the day with simplicity or extravagance. I like taking it easy, stepping back for a moment from all our electronic systems and letting my feet go for a stroll. Our research assistant poodle has helped us find some great morning walks that end with the best breakfasts in town. *sb*

Rosey's on Rogers

903 Rogers Street NW at Brawne Avenue NW
352.1103, www.roseysonrogers.com
Open: Su-M 8:30a-1:30p, Tu-Sa 8:30a-1:30p and 5:30-8:30p

Housed in an old corner store, Rosey's serves large plates of hearty breakfast fare to a loyal community. Regulars gather around the formica bar or sit under umbrellas on the terrace. In the summer, fragrant flowers fill the air before the marinated tempeh scramble or morel-stuffed omelet arrives at your table. Try buckwheat hazelnut pancakes for a more crunchy take on these syrup-doused favorites. I like mine with a mimosa, made here with fresh squeezed oranges and muddled mint. They have a small kitchen, so waits can be lingering, but they still manage larger groups, and have courteous staff who can juggle through the commotion. *sb*

New Moon Café

113 4th Avenue W at Capitol Way South
357.3452
Open: M-F 7a-2:30p, Sa 8a-2p
$ Vn Fr Fam CO

I love waking up at New Moon. Serving big mugs of B&B Coffee in a cozy sidewalk café, this is one of the most comforting breakfast joints in Oly. The benedicts are top-drawer—there is even a tofu benedict option. I recommend ordering anything you can douse in their homemade blackberry jam, conveniently served in a ketchup dispenser on every table. The buttermilk pancakes are always a sure thing and an egg sandwich will wake up every sleepy customer with its goodness. Recycling, composting and going organic, New Moon is as tasty as it is responsible. If you're around during the lunch hours, don't worry, breakfast is served all day. *dm*

Otto's

111 Washington Street NE at 4th Avenue E
352.8640
Open: M-Su 7a-6p
$ Veg Fr Fam

Breakfast at Otto's will brighten your day with an expansive, sunny interior and an extensive menu. Here bagels run the full-range of flavors, as do the spreads, including tofu and hummus. Otto's also has a full breakfast menu and a handful of sandwiches and salads to satisfy. San Francisco Street Bakery goods delight, and day-olds can also be picked up for reduced price. Look for the sign of a radiating sun of a bagel, and head in. A large area is allotted for flyers and postcards, so you just might discover a band playing this very night. *dm*

Capitol Lake, Heritage Park
5th Avenue SW at Water Street SW
Open: dawn to dusk

If a casual morning walk is all that can be sustained after a filling breakfast scramble, strolling from Percival Landing, past Heritage Fountain will bring wanderers to the grassy knoll on the northeast side of Capitol Lake. There's a walkway around the entire lake that can be taken altogether or in parts. Sometimes I just have to pinch myself when I see the breathtaking beauty of Olympia. One of my favorite vantage points is on the south side of Capitol Lake, past Heritage Park and Marathon Park, where a path winds its way up to the Capitol buildings, providing a perfect spot from which to view the lake, Budd Inlet, and the Olympic Mountains in the distance. I feel fortunate to be one of the lucky ones to take in this panorama first hand. *dm*

Darby's Café
211 5th Avenue SE at Washington Street SE
357.6229
Open: W-Sa 7a-9p Su 8a-9p
$-$$ Vn Fam

Located downtown, across from the Capitol Theater, Darby's Café is a reliable pick for breakfast or brunch. Always packed on the weekends, and closed on Monday and Tuesday, I suggest going to Darby's mid-week and sitting by the window. The eggs Benedict is very saucy, with a thick lemon-butter hollandaise. If you can't choose between breakfast and lunch, try the "In-between" sandwich, which is basically a chicken fried steak sandwich with eggs—not for the faint of heart. For a healthy choice, try the brewer's yeast tofu scramble, with tasty veggies. There are lots of vegetarian and vegan choices: vegan biscuits and gravy or the house-made veggie patties. Order the fresh squeezed orange juice for a cup of sunshine on a cloudy day. *pr*

Percival's Landing

Percival's Landing and Heritage Fountain
Between 4th Avenue Bridge and Thurston Avenue NE
Percival Landing offers the perfect place to enjoy simple pleasures in the morning hours: watching a hot cup of tea collecting steam on the window, the dewy grass on my bare-feet, and the tide going out as I walk along Olympia Pier before the town has woken up. My puppy and I start our walk at the Olympia Farmers Market. Dancing Goats coffee in hand, and Rainier cherries filling my pockets, I follow the wooden dock along the shore up to Heritage Fountain where kids are at play. Geysers shoot up from the ground in an unpredictable pattern, making it fun to parade across the fountain, with surprise of an upward water burst. Across the street I get an opportunity to lengthen my walk along Capitol Lake. *sb*

Blue Heron Bakery

4935 Mud Bay Road, west of Evergreen Parkway
866.2253, www.blueheronbakery.com
Open: M-Su 7a-6p

Even though Blue Heron's baked goods can be found all around Oly, I like to meet my friend Ellen at their bakery before a walk with doggie Dante. Their coffee is yummy, cold-press brewed, and the crowing glory, the baked goods, are something to write home about. I like their chocolate croissants because they solve that problem of un-even chocolate filling—there's some cocoa in every bite. It's worth the drive out of the center of town. *dm*

Madison Scenic Park

1600 10th Avenue SE between Central and Fir Streets SE

Owned by the Olympia School District, this landscaped park is perched on a hillside with views of the Black Hills and the Capitol Building. Walk along wood-railed paths and pass by wildflower patches on your morning walk above the city. The park itself isn't big enough for a long and leisurely stroll, so I recommend walking there from wherever you are staying, or from a nearby neighborhood if you want to get a little more morning action. *sb*

San Francisco Street Bakery

1320 San Francisco Avenue NE at Tullis Street NE
753.8553
Open: M-Sa 6:30a-7p, Su 6:30a-6p

San Francisco Street Bakery is the only place in Olympia where I feel truly comfortable writing in my journal. The side garden is a quiet sanctuary, complete with a wishing rock that catches rain. I sit next to the wide bay windows, looking out over the garden to the elementary school. I battle my way through Suduko puzzles, taking breaks to sip Earl Gray tea and bite my almond croissant, which makes everything seem luxurious. A toy kitchen next to the honey and milk always has some young pseudo-chef flinging fake pizza and dropping the bright plastic pans on the ground. Because their sandwiches are stuffed with hummus and sprouts and the soup of the day is always hearty, I can stay for as long as I need to with out worry of going hungry. Don't miss the heart-shaped hazelnut cookies, perched atop a big pastry case in a glass jar. Savor the moment by picking out a loaf of rosemary bread to take home. *pr*

Coffee Time

Coffee beans: ground, pressed, steeped and served

Batdorf and Bronson's Dancing Goats

Speaking as a true coffee person, I am overjoyed to find a city with local coffee roasters who are as obsessed with a good pour as I am. All locally owned, and very much entrenched in the community, these stops are frequented by a cross section of good Oly people who are in the know about organic and fair-trade coffee. Find coffee, tea and snacks, both sweet and savory, at these admirable cafés. Each offers its own unique ambiance and crowd; these coffee shops are indicators of what the surrounding neighborhood is like. *sb*

Dancing Goats Espresso
111 Market Street NE, across from the Farmers Market
528.8555, www.dancinggoats.com
Open: M-F 7a-5p Sa-Su 8a-5p

Batdorf and Bronson named their Market Street location in honor of the legend of the Dancing Goats—a tale of the discovery of coffee by a herd of goats who danced all night after eating the little shrub's berries. Modeled after the busy espresso bars in Italy, DG has a polished feel, friendly baristas, and window seating for people watching. All the beans are roasted right up the street and carted over. After a hot day shopping at the Farmers Market, I like to stop in for their humorously named Chilly Goat, the trademark blended coffee drink with a whip cream top. It's right on the DASH bus line, so you can get a free ride back up Capitol Way. *pr*

Olympia Coffee Roasting Company Cupping Room
203A 4th Avenue E at Washington Street SE
352.4628, www.olympiacoffeeroasting.com
Open: M-Sa 8a-5p

In this classic building sits the retail arm of the Olympia Coffee Roasting Company, a roaster that distributes its brews to many coffee shops in the area. Here a number of espresso, tea, and hot chocolate concoctions are ready to be sipped and there is also a small selection of baked treats to choose from, which makes it even more worth a stop in, if only to be absorbed in the deep colors and sharp style of the cupping room. For the connoisseurs seeking to sample Olympia's best, tastings can be arranged (see **City for Free** chapter). *dm*

Batdorf & Bronson

516 Capitol Way S at 5th Avenue SE
786-6717, www.batdorf.com
Open: M-F 6a-7p, Sa-Su 7a-6p
$ WiFi Fr S

A staple in the Olympia community since the mid-80's, Batdorf & Bronson (B&B) cups their own organic, fair-trade blends that go perfectly with a moment in one of their enveloping leather chairs. B&B goes out of their way to provide a relaxed atmosphere away from home for you to browse the paper or check your email on the free wireless Internet. This coffee roaster knows java and keeps it local with their solar-powered roastery, located right by the Farmers Market. With a yummy selection of pastries from which to choose and a long counter for long chats over steamy mugs. If you can't stay, take an Italian Soda in a to-go cup made from corn. I like stopping by B&B because there is always a friendly face, a chess game to watch, or a stranger to meet. *dm*

Mud Bay Coffee

1600 Cooper Point Road SW Suite 630
754.6222, www.mudbaycoffeeco.com
Open: M-F 6a-6p, Sa-Su 8a-6p
$ Vn Fr S

Rare is the café that can in good conscience be proposed as an ally in the battle against sleeplessness. Nevertheless, patrons of Mud Bay Coffee can sleep better at night knowing they're not satisfying their caffeine fix at the expense of honest, hard-working farmers. By developing direct relationships with small farms around the world, Mud Bay Coffee and its local suppliers ensure that their farmers always earn a respectable wage. All their coffee is roasted daily, filling the place with a delicious and comforting scent. A fireplace in the corner invites you to lose an afternoon in their cozy chairs with a beverage in your right hand and a book, perhaps this book, in your left hand. They offer scrumptious baked goods from a variety of local bakeries, host local musicians, and feature the work of a local artist each month throughout the cafe, exemplifying their commitment to promoting the local culture. *mr*

Caffé Vita

Caffé Vita Coffee Roasting Company
124 4th Avenue E at Capitol Way S
754-8187, www.caffevita.com
Open: M-Su 7a-8p
$ WiFi Fr S

Caffé Vita Olympia was started in Seattle, but the Olympia store is a central fixture of the 4th Avenue strip. Sourcing coffee from the Americas, Indonesia, and Africa, Caffé Vita brews up cups that are dark and earthy, acidic and fruity. With Blue Heron Bakery munchies from which to pick from and rotating artwork to peruse, the ambiance is clean and comfortable. The community board will let you know what is happening around town and the soothing sounds on the speakers will ease you into the next escapade. *dm*

The Filling Station Espresso
728 4ᵗʰ Avenue E at Plum Street
754.8415
Open: M-Sa 6a-6p, Su 7a-5p
Driving along the West Coast, you'll see drive-thru coffee shops littering the roadsides on nearly every route. I don't know if there is a support group for caffeine addicts, but membership would fill up fast in this neck of the woods. There's nothing more immediate than purchasing your daily fix without leaving the driver's seat of your car. The Filling Station is an especially noteworthy addition to this group—with the feel of an old-thyme gas station that would grace the canvas of like an Edward Hopper painting. *dm*

Artisans Community Entertainment Café
109 N Capitol Way at 4ᵗʰ Avenue E
www.theartisancafe.com
Open: M-Sa 9a-11p, Su 10a-6p
Artisans is a new addition to the coffee spots around town. This musical café has a complete with performance space and a balcony where you can wax creative over a cup (and saucer) of fair trade coffee. To satisfy your sweet tooth try their "black keys and ivory," a mix of white and milk hot chocolate with a dash of espresso. Local bakery items contribute to the overflowing food case, and make great sides with one of the salad bowls made with organic ingredients. *sb*

Do Lunch

Outstanding mid-day eating of every sort

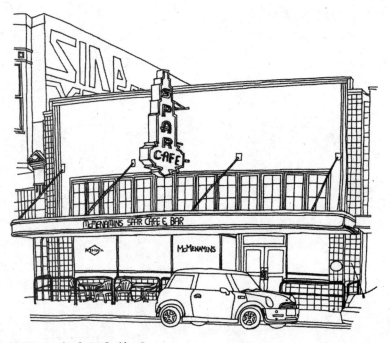

McMenamins Spar Café & Bar

Lunch is my favorite meal of the day. When I lived in Switzerland, it was an event, with several courses and mandatory attendance by the entire family. In fact, some parts of the world consider this the largest meal of the day, accompanied by a siesta. There are many types of lunches— savoring something from the Farmer's Market foodcarts, a Cadillac burrito at QB or a bay-side sandwich made to your specifications. Even though I've avoided the typical "eat" or "restaurant" sections typical of other guidebooks, and incorporated food into various chapters, I had to dedicate a spot for lunch. From business power lunches to lazy afternoon munching, it's a state of mind. *sb*

McMenamins Spar Café & Bar
114 4ᵗʰ Avenue NE at Captol Way S
357.6444, www.sparcafe.com
Open: M-Sa 7a-12a
$$ Veg Fr

For over 65 years the Spar Café has offered its dinner style food to Olympia's working class. Although politicians have mostly replaced the lumberjacks, the food is still fit for any good-ol' boy. There are plenty of cozy booths to choose from or a long J-shaped lunch counter to perch at, with swiveling chairs each equipped with their own hat-hook. A beautiful building; be sure to notice all the finer details of the craftsmanship. Water from the artesian well beneath the Spar is used to brew McMenamins trademark beer, Sunflower IPA. *jp*

Oskar's German and European Deli
720-H Sleater-Kinney Road SE, Lacey
491.3251
Open: M-F 9a-6p, Sa 9a-5p
$ Fam CO

For your next foray into the parks of South Sound, why not bring non-traditional picnic fare like homemade bratwurst, Bockwurst of Knackwurst. Neatly packaged box lunches make the best sauerkraut and sausages in the area highly portable. Call your order in ahead of time and you can swing by on your way to your next adventure. Don't get over-hungry on a full day of Olympia explorations ever again. *sb*

Sidewalk Cafe
601 Capitol Way N at B Avenue E
956.7189
Open: Everyday, 8a-2p
$ Veg Dg

Located half a block up Capitol from the farmers market, Sidewalk cafe is the place to go if the market closes and you are still hungry. They have cold soups and salads to go, and zingy ginger cookies. I take my turkey avocado sandwich with zesty chipolatas mayonnaise out to their seating area or over to Percival landing. Look for the tin spaceship perched on top of this cute blue deli. *pr*

Angels Thai Cuisine
318 4th Avenue E at Franklin Street SE
786.1252
Open: M-W 11a-9p, Th-F 11a-10p, Sa 4p-10
$-$$ Fr Fam Vn

Angels does up their Thai just the way you want it-- comforting, in plenty and with the optional kick of Thai spicy for the brave and strong taste buds. Their $7.50 lunch menu is a good midday option. I recommend the Pad Kee Mao for some sweetness and those wonderfully wide noodles. The shrimp appetizer is uniquely battered in crunchy fried noodles and a good challenge to avoid making a mess. This is the place for the cholesterol-free diner, with over 20 vegan menu options to choose from. *dm*

Traditions Café and World Folk Art
300 5th Avenue SW at Water Street SW
705.2819, www.traditionsfairtrade.com
Open: M-F 9a-6p, Sa 10a-6p
$ Fr Fam Vn

Traditions serves up food with a side of fair trade goods and community activism. This is a hybrid joint, joining a large café room for diners, gatherings of local community groups and musical performances with a shop that sells everything from organic socks and teamwork toys to books like 'A People's History of the United States'. A hotbed of activity, there is usually something 'political' going on at Traditions and there are always inexpensive lunch items to fill up the activists. Head here to get motivated to action, check out a book from the lending library or pick up some Olympic Mountain Ice Cream for gallivanting at Capitol Lake right across the street. *dm*

Meconi's Italian Subs of Olympia
1051 Capitol Way S at Legion Way
543.0240, www.meconissubs.com
Open: M-F 10a-7p, Sa 10a-8p
$ Veg Fr Fam

After a high school swim practice I felt as if I could eat the entire contents of my boarding school cafeteria. I kept trying to recreate the perfect hoagie, but in my over-zealous hunger usually mash a mish mosh. Meconi's makes the classic, East Coast hoagie without ingredient overload. A special oil blend is sprinkled on every sandwich that's ordered "regular" so don't let them skip it on yours. I like the creamy egg salad, the peppery corn beef or the nitrite-free smoked turkey. A whole sandwich stuffs two hungry people. *sb*

Vic's Pizzeria
233 Division Street NW at Harrison Avenue NW
943.8044
Open: M-Sa 8a-9p
$ Fr S Vn

Growing up on the East Coast, whenever we didn't know what we wanted for dinner, pizza was our fail-safe. It was floppy, greasy, and crispy all at the same time and we would fold up slice after cheesy slice in adolescent delight, shaking our heads at the girls sopping up the fattening grease with paper towels and running the dangerous risk of the cheese sticking to the paper and being drawn up with the grease. My standards are high for pizza and my West Coast fail-safe is Thai food for a reason. But in Vics, I have finally found a reliable pizza option, with a crispy crust that puts other pizza joints to shame. My recent penchant for the cholesterol-free options of the world has me ecstatic with Vics' stellar vegan slices and gigantic vegan calzone. The checkered floor, bulletin boards filled with dog photos and concert posters hung on the walls create a comforting atmosphere and the correctly cooked pies all help make Vics a beloved pizza place. Plus, some claim that their vegan chocolate cake is the best dessert in town. *dm*

California Taco
Two Taco Trucks:
Sleater-Kinney Boulevard between 6th & 7th Avenues
Harrison Avenue just past Kenyon Street
$ Dg PW Fr

Also know as "taco trailers" or "the burrito buses", these Burrito carts showed up 3 years ago and Olympia hasn't been the same since. The fleet of carts are run by the Moreno family, who also run the Mayan Family Mexican Restaurant in Lacey. I don't know about you, but I love to shoot the shit with a bunch of hungry friends in a cute little parking lot while waiting for my grub. Big messy veggie or meat burritos for 6 dollars, or tacos for 1.50 each. I like to get the bottled coca cola with real sugarcane to wash it all down. *pr*

Curry in a Hurry
at the Olympia Farmer's Market
April-Aug Th-Su 10a-3p
$ S PW

If you are in a hurry, grab a plate of curry, but take the time to sit down and fully enjoy its deep hearty flavor. In the summer I go for the mouth-watering mango lassi, in the winter months I warm up with their homemade chai tea. For a side try the packoras (made with chickpea flour) or a veggie-packed samosa. Most of the dishes are vegan, and go wonderfully with a weekend musical offering at the nearby stage. *pr*

Bayview Deli
516 4th Avenue W at Percival Landing
352.4901
Open: Everyday, 6a-12a
$-$$ Fam Veg Dg

Bayview's Sandwich counter offers fancy cold salads that I like to sample, then go home and try to recreate. Plus the selections change often enough that you can go every week and still be wowed. They have many interesting sandwiches to pick from, including brie and pesto, so its embarrassing to admit that I order the chicken salad on rye every time, packed full of sprouts and tomato. With my brown bag to go, complete with a pickle and a bag of chips, I feel just like a kid at summer camp. Exit out the back door for a view of the Olympics. *pr*

Fifth Avenue Sandwich Shop
117 5th Avenue SE at Capitol Way S
705.3393
Open: M-Sa 10a-7p
$ Fr Fam

This Family owned sandwich shop is just the place to stop in for a good old-fashioned sandwich. Eat in the cozy comfort of their dimly lit booths, or take your sammy (West coast speak for sandwich) to go and walk to Sylvester Park. All the bread is made from scratch in store, and so are the pies, cookies, and the hugest cinnamon rolls you will ever enjoy in Olympia or elsewhere. The Ruben is hot and melty yet retains its crispness. The egg salad is nice simple classic, yet could use some extra something. Ask for a pickle and pepper! *sb*

The Bread Peddler
222 Capitol Way N at State Avenue NE
352.1175
Open: Tu-F 7a-6p, Sa 7a-4p
$$ Veg PW

Whenever I'm walking along Capitol Way during that late lunch hour I have a tough decision to make. Should I order the tuna niçoise or the blue cheese roast beef sandwich at Bread Peddler. Life is tough! The robustness of chevre and oven roasted tomatoes atop a perfectly young leafy bed make a cresh for sherry tuna salad. On the other hand, horseradish ailoi spread on their own focaccia bread with melt-in-you-mouth crumbles of blue cheese are blissful with rare roast beef. I may never make up my mind, but one thing is for sure, which ever sandwich I choose I'll leave with a little satchel of pastries in hand for doling out to deserving friends or stashing for my next work break. Eat up, I bid you! *sb*

Hang Out

All the best chill out spots, from a cozy reading nook to a relaxed microbrew with your buddies.

King Solomon's Reef

Sometimes the best way to get a sense of a place is to slow down and stop attempting to see everything and do everything. Try a new board game at Ben Moore's or a walk through the mists of Decatur Woods Park and give new meaning to loitering. Olympia has a very relaxed pace; it's a place where you can put life on hold for a moment to enjoy the simple things—see beauty in rain drops and wax poetic in your journal. Bring friends or venture out alone for a moment off the treadmill of usual livelihood. *sb*

King Solomon's Reef
212 4th Avenue W at Jefferson Street NE
357.5552
Open: Everyday, 6a-2a
$ Fr Veg
Hungry and drunk at one in the morning isn't always the best situation in which to find yourself. But if this occurs at Reef, your picture is a bit brighter. After all, it is the place "where fun goes when you sleep." I'm out of that scene now, but I once had my gin and tonic pried away promptly at 2a. The baskets of hamburgers, melts and fries took away the collective sting of being cut off. With a long row of booths opposite the counter and kitchen, local art displayed on the high-reaching walls, and a bar tucked away in the back, the Reef has suave diner style. And for those who make it to the Reef before midnight, I highly recommend ordering any and all of the pie a la mode you can get. It's made by someone's mother with love, and it really hits the spot. *pr*

Westside Lanes
2200 Garfield Avenue NW
943.2400
Open: Tu-Su 12-11p
I've been bowling at Westside Lanes for years and although I've never broken 100, I still have a great time, every time. The food is good, so if you're hungry order a big basket of nachos and some soda to get the full bowling-ally experience. One-dollar shoe rentals, well-oiled lanes and great selection of fancy bowling balls to choose from, locally-owned Westside Lanes makes me feel a bowling princess. *pr*

Tugboat Annie's
2100 Westbay Drive NW
943.1850, www.tugboatannies.com
Th 11a-9p F-Sa 11a-10p
$$ Veg Fr

Located above the quieter side of Olympia's Bud Inlet, Tugboat Annie's is a great place to watch the boats bob side to side at the dock. Locals drift in and out of the restaurant, lounging the patio as they gulp pints of beer from Fishtail Brewery. The portions are made for large appetites—one afternoon I watched in amazement as my friend Ben devoured his steak, sides and beers, and then helped me with my blue cheese mushroom burger. Try the fish and chips, made from freshly caught cod. *pr*

Decatur Woods Park
Decatur Street SW and 11th Avenue SW
753-8380, www.ci.olympia.wa.us

On misty afternoons I don my rain gear and Wellies, and head to Decatur Woods where the magic of the forest abounds. Follow a maze of nature trails through the temperate rainforest. If you want to hang for longer, pick up some tasty grain salads from Olympia Food Co-op and take a seat at one of the roofed picnic benches for an outdoor meal. Decatur Woods gives me the escape I need and a chance to munch on my specialty GORP mix: dried coconuts, pineapple, sunflower seeds, cashews and peanut butter chips— ironically no raisins or peanuts in my signature mix. *sb*

Oly Rollers
Skateland
1200 Southbay Road NE
352.9943, www.skateland.com, www.olyrollers.com

Roller Derby bouts are a spectacle of cringe-inspiring collisions where cute (but tough) women don old-school roller skates to duke it out on the rink. The Oly Rollers face off against teams from around the country as well as more local opponents, like Portland's Rose City Rollers and Bend's Lava City Roller Dolls who assert, 'It's better to get knocked down than knocked up!' A word play on Olympia Beer's slogan 'Its the water!' the Oly Rollers chant, 'Its the slaughter!' And slaughter they do! The Oly Rollers host a number of events besides bouts, so check out their website to see what's happening. *pr*

Ben Moore's Café

112 4th Avenue at Capitol Way
357.7527
Open: M 11a-8p, Tu-Th 11a-9p, F 11a-10p, Sa-Su 9a-2p 5-9p
Bar Open: Su-F 5p-2a, Sa 6p-2a
$ Veg Fr

The back of Ben Moore's offers cozy seating, entertainment provided. But if no band is rocking the joint, choose from the hoard of board games, and grab a few pints for you and your Scrabble crew. Hang out for hours of game-board fun and tipsy giggles. If you are hungry you can order heaps a heaping order of fries or a hearty sandwich will to save your grumbling tummy. I like to play my own versions of games like tackling the Scrabble board in French. When that gets old, play the dictionary game by picking up the dictionary, and choosing a tricky word. Each person makes up their own definition, then takes a turn reading the invented meanings along with the real one and whoever chooses the true definition gets a point—a simple and potentially hilarious game. Low prices and a laid back Olympia crowd makes this spot a true favorite. *sb*

The Royal

311 N Capitol Way
705.0760, www.theroyalolympia.com
Open: M-Su 4p-2a
$ Fr S

In the rain or when the sun has sunk below the horizon, it can be hard to find a glow. At those moments when my energy is in danger of rapidly waning I go for a round of bocce ball at The Royal. Even though lines are rare in Oly, The Royal often has a trail of eager folks waiting at the bar for their luscious fruity drinks, made with organic fruit juices, or their well-done standards. Located in a restored warehouse and filled with tawny vintage furniture, The Royal allows groups of friends to relax in the homey-ness of a large comfortable living room. Join in conversation as though at a friend's house, or a friend of a friend's for that matter. Don't skip at least a quick flip through at the stellar juke box—it is the best one in town. Hip bartenders and a good mix of people make this our favorite new bar. Happy hours from 4-7p mean two-dollar well drinks and a buck-fifty for Oly Beer. *sb*

Capitol Campus
Capitol Way and 11th Avenue
586.3460, www.ga.wa.gov/visitor

Olympians have a propensity for slowing down and enjoying the simple pleasures in life. In springtime the light pink snow-fields of cherry blossoms that edge the Capitol campus bring a flood of lawn-picnic-ers. With the soft sound of a huge bubbling fountain and monuments of democracy overhead, the large lawn in front of the State Capitol building is the best spot in town for finding pictures in the clouds. Walking tours are available every day of the week, so tour the main Legislative Building's regal 278-foot-high dome, and bring your own picnic blanket and a book and you'll be all set to relax. *pr/dm*

Fish Tale Brew-Pub
515 Jefferson Street SE at Legion Way
943.3650, www.fishbrewing.com
Open: M-Sa 11a-12a, Su 12-10p
$ Veg Fr S

Beer enthusiasts will be intrigued to note that the headquarters of Fish Tale Ales, one of the Northwest's more respected microbreweries, is located in downtown Olympia. Of even greater interest is the fact that the Fish Tale Brewery operates its own brewpub, known as the Fishbowl. This is an excellent place to come when you want to de-tox from youth culture; sedate and mature, the Fishbowl is popular with old hippies, folk musicians, bearded nautical types and outdoorsy people. Enter a muraled building across from the brewery itself, where steal casks boldly labeled 'organic hops' stand proudly by the street. Sit at the bar to ham it up with the friendliest bar tenders in town and learn more about their stellar brews. I love the creamy porter. For something drier I go for the pilsner or special Winterfish and for those moments when you need an extra jolt, I recommend the Monkfish Belgian, a whopping 8.5%. In addition to the selections from the Fish Tale Brewery next door, there's also a rotating selection of guest beers. Creative Northwestern cuisine is available from the kitchen at reasonable prices, from small snacks to full dinners. Share a plate of nachos made with organic corn chips, local sharp cheddar and heaps of homemade salsa. They make a different soup each day, and you can order it with half a sandwich for a bargain. *sb/jp*

Eastside/Clubside Café

410 4th Avenue E
357.9985, www.theeastsideclub.com
Open: M-F 12p-2a, Sa-Su 1p-2a
$ Vn Dg WiFi

The Eastside has a reputation as something of a hippie bar, and to be sure there's almost certain to be at least one person in there at any given time with a giant head-full of dreadlocks or a fairly-traded skirt made from hemp by unionized Guatemalan peasants. The fact, though, is that the Eastside occupies a place very dear to the heart of just about everyone who passes through its doors, for the simple reason that it's one of the best damn bars in town. Lined up behind the counter are more beer taps than you've probably ever seen assembled in one place, each pulling a different delicious microbrew. In the back you'll find multiple pool tables as well as ping-pong, Foosball, air hockey, darts, and vintage video games. One of the best things about the Eastside is the window into the kitchen of the Clubside Cafe next door, through which you can order from a large menu of classic bar food. There's also a jukebox, and to top it all off there's a retro 50's laundromat in the back so you can bend your elbow at the bar whilst you launder your undies! On Fridays and Saturdays there's often live music; the space is particularly well-frequented by bluegrass or old-time music bands. *jp*

Skateland

1200 Southbay Road NE
352.9943, www.skatelandolympia.com
Open: Tu 6:30-8:30p, W 1-4p, 7-9p, Th 1-4p, F-Sa 7-11p

I hope I'm never too grown up to think that roller-skating is just for kids. Over the years I've had so much "kid-fun" at Skateland in my "adult-life" over the years: Paige and I playing leapfrog until someone falls down, Shizuno leading a game of red-light green-light—once my friend Isaac actually threw his body down in my path to try to trip me! When I tire of skating, I sneak into the black and white photo booth to document my glowing mood. Skateland also offers slushies and air-hockey for those who shy away from skating. Wednesday is dollar night, and don't forget to look for flyers of upcoming Roller Derby matches of the Oly Rollers. *pr*

Casual Night Out

Dining and delighting in a relaxed atmosphere.

Water Street Café

There is always a time when you just want to kick back and have a relaxed evening out. The state of Washington is blanketed with a rich natural beauty, which just might have give the people reason enough to stay casual most of the time—let nature do the dressing up! Go out, but go in comfort, with the divine purpose of repose. Good eats and good laughs galore lie ahead. *sb*

Water Street Café

610 Water Street SW at Legion Way SE
709.9090, www.waterstreetcafeandbar.com
Open: M-Th 11a-9p, F 11a-10p, Sa 4:30-10p, Su 4:30-9p
$$-$$$ Veg Ro

The Water Street Café is Olympia's only restaurant with a real "big city" feel. Here you'll be immersed in a clean posh atmosphere; every time I go I get a little gussied up. The mystery secret ingredient in the crab cakes turns out to be mayonnaise, but it is made in-house from the eggs of farm raised hens eggs. The Polpettone al Forno, Italian meat loaf, is a classic recipe done exceptionally well here. Their lamb salad is great, or for those desiring rich food try the squash tortellini served doused in luxurious cream sauce and topped with tangy cheese and toasted hazelnuts. Choose what catches your eye, the chef has come up with consistent elegant fare. After all, this place makes even mayo taste fancy! *pr*

Urban Onion Restaurant

116 Legion Way SE at Washington Street SE
943.9242
Open: M-Th 7a-9p, F 7a-10p, Sa 8a-10p, Su 8a-9p
$$ Veg Fam

Originally called the "Herb & Onion," Olympia's West Coast slang quickly condensed "Herb and" to "Urban." Located in the Olympian Hotel, the Urban Onion is a cozy place to warm up in winter. I like to get their lentil soup with house-made bread and salad. In additional to an expansive vegetarian menu boasting hummus, zingy bean dips and ravioli, the Urban Onion has great seafood and burgers. Check out the back of the restaurant, which turns into a bar at night. *pr*

Le Voyeur
404 4th Avenue E at Adams Street SE
943.5710
Open: M-Su 11:30-2a
$ Vn Fr PW

If you have multiple tongue piercings, answer to 'ze' rather than traditional gendered pronouns, have a deliberately asymmetrical hairstyle, play in an indie rock synth-pop band, or consider yourself a well-informed radical anarchist, then you'll feel right at home at Le Voyeur, "where the young feel old and the old feel young." If none of the above apply, you'll probably feel fairly comfortable all the same; it's a friendly sort of a place. Have a seat in the uniquely-decorated front dining room if you intend to order food; waits can be long but the cooking is superb and there are plenty of vegetarian and vegan options. Otherwise head to the bar in back, past the walk-in fridge stocked with a dazzling array of bottled beers. Proceed even further to the rear of the establishment and you'll eventually get to the performance space. More often than not you'll find a free show in progress featuring local or touring indie rock bands. The noteworthy exception are Wednesdays. Wednesday night is Trivia Night at Le Voyeur—your opportunity to match wits with a panel of talented experts, putting everything at stake in the hopes of winning stupendous prizes beyond your wildest dreams. It's hilarious, entertaining, and not to be missed. *jp*

Koibito Japanese Restaurant
1707 Harrison Avenue NW at Black Lake Boulevard SW
352.4751
Open M-F 11a-10p, Sa-Su 4-10p
$$ Veg Fr

On hot summer nights, the people of the Westside flock to Koibito for sushi rolls and mochi. The house special Koibito Roll is amazing; cream cheese makes a smooth companion for seared tuna. Halfway through the Koibito Roll I cannot hold it in anymore and I loudly exclaim, "I feel healthier already!", which is what good sushi should do for you. Koibito also treats us to fresh ginger, not that dyed pink stuff. The wasabi is nice and sharp, just don't breath in through your nose when you get too much of it! After the dusted green tea mochi are all eaten up, our kind and talented sushi chef brings us a little orange boat with an umbrella. *pr*

Rambling Jacks

520 4th Avenue E at Eastside Street NE
754.8909, www.ramblingjacks.com
Open: Tu-Th 11a-10p, F–Sa 11a-11p, Su-M 11a-9p
$$ Fr Fam Veg

I went to Rambling Jacks for lunch with my roommate Carson, the pizza hound. Our applewood-fired pizzas arrived just in time to save us from spoiling our appetites on the yam fries, which aren't on the menu, but ask for them anyway and they'll be brought to your table in a flash. His veggie pizza was a perfect garden of color with a grassy base made of pesto sauce; my BBQ chicken pizza smelled like an onion in cilantro heaven. Everything was happily consumed except for one slice that Carson ate in the car on the drive home. We used the three different bottles of BBQ sauce on our table to spruce up our slices—not that our pizza needed any sprucing. Gigantic salads and classic American fare fill out the menu, which is the size of the Sunday New York Times. *pr*

Quality Burrito

113 4th Avenue W at Plum Street SE
357.3452
Open: Su-Th 6p-12a, F-Sa 6-11p
$ Fr Veg PW

Quality Burrito is the burrito headquarters of this capitol town. The menu reads a little like the funny pages, honoring the peculiarities of all kinds of icons. Gaze at an oily portrait of Michael Jackson while attempting to finish a Cadillac—a stuffed burrito that's crispy fried on the outside and divinely gushy on the inside. Don't leave without dessert because their homemade caramel is some of the best I have ever had. They drizzle heaps of it over fried banana wontons and vanilla bean ice cream. Pile in one of their vinyl booths with a gaggle of friends or chirping younguns' for heaps of cheap eats. *sb*

Fuji Japanese Restaurant
214 4th Avenue W near Water Street SE
352.0306
Open: M-Th 11a-9p, F-Sa 11a-9p, Su 3-8p
$ Veg Fr PW

Located near the boardwalk and 4th Avenue Bridge, Fuji is a great place to sit and watch people pour into downtown Olympia. The Chicken Teriyaki is cheap and served in deliciously large portions. The same goes for the noodle dishes; I recommend ordering the Yaki Udon with pork. The sushi is tasty and fresh, and much of the fish and shellfish is sourced locally. My favorite specialty roll, The Fuji Special Roll, is a balance of smooth, crispy and plump textures with avocado, deep-fried prawns and crab. Go during sunset for the best view—a platter of sushi perfectly compliments the glowing clouds over Budd Inlet. *pr*

Mini Saigon
111 Columbia Street NW at State Avenue NW
709.0854
Open: Everyday, 11a-9p
$$ Vn Fam

In a city where Thai food restaurants abound, Mini Saigon provides a never-ending menu to explore. Although they may not be serve the best Pad Thai in the world, its low price, large quantity, and perfect balance of spices has won it my lifetime loyalty. For a light lunch I combine the vegan wonton soup (with juicy Seitan) and the egg-roll spring rolls. That's right—the freshness of spring rolls doesn't mean being cheated out of a deep-fried shrimp egg roll, its in the mix with fresh bean sprouts and addictive peanut sauce. All spring I wait in anticipation of the summer mango salad. Sumi paintings of kittens and horses on the walls, tall glasses of sweet, dark Thai iced tea, and its proximity to Percival landing all contribute to Mini Saigon's greatness. *pr*

Jakes on 4th Avenue

311 4th Avenue E at Adams Street SE
956.3247
Open: M-Su 4p-2a

Unlike some gay bars, Jakes on 4th welcomes everyone with its fun atmosphere, "come as you are" attitude and living-the-good-life music selection. Jakes is a great place to play hide and seek—the floor plan includes three main levels: pool tables are up by the bar, booths line the dance floor, and there is the stage for drag shows and ultra-fabulous karaoke. Jakes is understanding when it comes to the nicotine set, when the ban started they made a back door section for where smokers huddle around no matter what the weather. *sb/pr*

Mercato

111 Market Street NE at Franklin Street NE
528.3663, www.mercatoristorante.com
Open: Su-M 11a-9p, Tu-Sa 11a-10:30p
$$$ Veg Fr Fam Dg

If you're in the mood for Italian but want something a bit more upscale and elaborate than Trinachria, the Mercato (named for its proximity to the Olympia Farmers Market) offers creative and delicious food, excellent cocktails, fine wines, succulent deserts, and rich after-dinner coffee from the nearby Batdorf and Bronsen Roastery. Vegetarian options are plentiful, and the butternut squash ravioli is an exceptionally good choice. The Mercato is a particularly nice place to meet for lunch after a morning at the Farmers Market. The prices are reasonable considering the quality and quantity of the food and the care that's taken with service and presentation. The Mercato is definitely a cloth-napkins-and-white-tablecloth sort of a place and you should be prepared to spend accordingly. Be advised as well that the main dining area can be a bit clamorous and you might want to specifically request an isolated table, or a spot on your patio if you're hoping for some quiet, intimate chit-chat. *jp*

Lemon Grass Restaurant
212 4th Avenue W at Capitol Way S
705.1832
Open: M-F 11a-2p and 5-9p, Sa 12-9p
$$ Veg Ro Fr

Everywhere I turn in the Pacific Northwest, there is another Thai place, each touting that they are the best at what they do. I've struggled through gluey noodles, rock hard veggies and overly creamy sauces and was ready to throw up my hands and give up until all my Olympia pals directed me to the Thai restaurant of their heart: Lemongrass. Owned by a friendly local couple and situated in the downtown corridor, this unassuming spot is a magestic homage to its native cuisine. Even though the wife co-owner is Vietnamese, she knows all about Thai food and has made the classics shine. If you are two, order luxurious honey walnut shrimp and the Mix Barbecue Vietnamese Style that comes with shrimp and pork and an assortment of basil, sprouts, veggies and spring rolls to stuff into make-your-own wraps. Just dip the rice wrappers in the hot water for a moment so they are malleable and roll up the stuffings to your heart's desire. The Pad Thai is pleasing, but I'd rather the green curry, the best curry on their long menu, which can be made vegan or for meat eaters. Come with a group of friends and squeeze into a booth under sewn paintings of life in Thailand. The verdict is back; for a great casual night out Olympians are dazzled by Lemongrass. *sb*

Old School Pizzeria
108 Franklin Street NE at State Avenue NE
786.9640
Open: M-Th 11a-10p, F-Sa 11a-11p, Su 12:30-10p
$ Veg Fr Fam PW

Although the punk kids behind the counter go out of their way to make my pizza just right, the Pac-Man machine and mod posters tend to distract me from my meal. Pizza by the slice are served steaming hot, so get a cool Mirror Pond Pale Ale to balance things out. Sit at the counter or call in your order ahead to take a pizza present to your friends and family. *sb/pr*

Cebu Restaurant

9408 Martin Way E #4
455.9128, www.cebuwa.com
Open: M-F 11a-9p, Sa 12-9p
$-$$ Fr Ro Veg

It might take a couple of U-turns to actually end up at Cebu—this unassuming Filipino restaurant is situated in a strip mall that abuts a Texaco gas station and only a dingy sign hints that it's a destination dining locale. But every time I'm in town I make a point of dining here, U-turns or no. The kitchy yet imaginative décor has a way of whisking me away to an island paradise, a major plus with the clouds are heavy outside. Put simply, Cebu's inspired food is tasty, unique and affordable, plus the chef/owner is cheerful and easy going. Baboy (pork), baka (beef), pagkaing dagat (seafood) and manok (chicken) dishes are all delectable options, but the traditional Filipino meal, Ginataang Langka, offers the chance to dine on jackfruit, one of the largest (if not *the* largest) fruit in the world, which tastes a bit like chicken in this particular rendition. It's never easy finding such a hidden gem, but Cebu is truly a buried treasure. *sb/dm*

The Mark

407 Columbia Street SW at State Avenue NE
754.4414, www.themarkolympia.com
Open: Th-Sa 5p-2a
$$$ Veg Ro Fr

When I go into The Mark, I always feel underdressed. The eloquent yet chic atmosphere, the handsome bartenders, and the mood lighting combine to make a nonverbal joke out of my rumpled dress and beat-up sandals. But have no fear! Outside on the back patio I find my friends, sitting around huge picnic tables like kids at camp, enjoying drinks and appetizers with good-humored horseplay. I always order the chocolate cake, which tastes like a thin slice of heaven, made with fair trade cocoa. For something more substantial, come for a fish dinner. Heralded as the best fish in town, The Mark buys its fish from the only solar powered fishing company in the US, and cooks it simply and with class, in their tradition of rustic food without pretense. *pr*

Oyster House
320 4th Avenue W near Water Street SW
753.7000, www.olympiaoysterhouse.com
Open: Su-Th 11a-10p, F-Sa 11a-11p
$$ Fam Fr

The most convenient place for local oysters is the old oyster shucking hut-turned restaurant, the Oyster House. Steeped in Olympia history, this place has been very dolled up to the point where it has an almost institutional feel, but the fried clams are still jammin'. Get your fill of fried seafood here, or opt for oven-baked fish served with homemade coleslaw. When the weather permits, take a seat on the porch, perched right above the Sound. Even if you not that hungry, this is a great locale for a warm drink, and an oyster shooter snack. *sb*

Gardener's Seafood & Pasta
111 Thurston Avenue NW at Washington Street NE
786.8466
Open: Tu-Sa 5-9p
$$$ Ro Veg

The romance icon in our key just doesn't do Gardener's justice. The cozy dinning room is intimate, the exposed rafters remind of rolling around in the hay. My last anniversary meal was here—our waitress tucked us in to one of two and raised platforms with single tables, where we watched the privacy of a bungalow, plus a great view. The menu is packed with local foods, sourced from some of the farms in the **Farm to Table** chapter. I savored my upscale seafood burrito that was richly packed with crab and a bouquet of mollusks. My beloved silently devoured his tri-tip steak and mashed potatoes, which were divinely silky. Save room for the homemade desserts, made for feeding each other across the table. *pr*

Italian Restaurants

Sorrentos Restaurant
430 Legion Way SE at Cherry Street SE
352.9915
Open: M-F 11a-2p and 5-10p, Sa 5-10p
$$ Fam Veg

An impressive painted façade towers above classically Italian Cinzano umbrellas and tables with checkered table clothes. Inside, two-tops flank the windows with large tables deeper in the room for family gatherings. Franco, the owner and cheerleader of Sorrentos, is always smiling and ready to take orders. Franco's picture is featured twice in the menu and he is definitely the shtick of the joint. He jokingly refers to himself as feisty as he playfully pats his customers on the shoulder, and he seems to have his hand in all the operations at Sorrentos, a restaurant that fills the East Coast Italian restaurant role well. The food is solid American-Italian and includes one of my favorites, Penne Campagnola, covered in flavorful tomato sauce with locally-made sausage and grilled shrimp. Another house specialty is the sublime baked ziti. The wine list outdoes the food menu in length by an entire page and features expensive hard to find vintages with Wine Spectator scores as high as 99. Sorrentos will satisfy that odd yearning we all secretly have for a paternalistic Italian restaurant. *sb/dm*

Portofino Ristorante
101 Division Street NW near Walnut Road NW
352.2803
Open: M-Su 430-9p
$$-$$$ Ro Fr Veg

Portofino creates an air of sophistication while maintaining its relaxed ambiance. With many enclaves and alcoves to settle into at this house-based restaurant, I love the intimate vibe; often the place will feel like it serves you and your companion alone— sometimes this might actually be the case. The menu features a Dungeness crab cake appetizer that rises above expectations—four thick, beautifully flavored cakes have been spared over-frying. There are many unique pasta and meat entrees to choose from, the clam pasta is delectable. A glass or two of wine and a subtle slide into a molten chocolate soufflé dessert complete an evening of sensual eating. *dm*

Trinacria Ristorante Italiano
113 Capitol Way N at State Avenue NE
352.8892
Open: M-Sa 11:30a-1p and 5:30-9p
$$ Ro Fr R

Even though Olympia is a stately city, its idealism and revolving businesses make the scene rather new. Older businesses aren't prevailing over new ventures that focus on people's current needs and fascinations. Eugenio and his restaurant Trinacria have cut right through the norm having stayed open and happening for over 20 years. I don't know where to begin—the calzone (please pronounce it right when ordering, calzoney, or you might get a slap on the back of the hand) is the most perfect incarnation of this double sided pizza. Sit by the fire in this tiny one-room transport to Sicily and peruse the wine list. The food menu never has a gargantuan number of choices, but when you walk through the door, you are walking into the chef's hands. You'll find locals and people who've driven all the way from Seattle to taste the hand made tortellini, seafood pasta, and of course tiramisu for desert. *sb*

Basilico Ristorante Italiano

507 Capitol Way S #A at 5th Street SE
570.8777 www.ristorantebasilico.com
Open: M-Sa 12-2p and 5-9p
$$$ Ro Veg

With a wall of wine bottles and a pasta counter, Basilico's atmosphere is smart and comfortable. Although I'm not a huge fan of shellfish, the Italian Rivera Tagliatelle clams doused in plum tomato sauce were hard to resist at my last trip here, with a table of friends and roomies. Traditional fettuccine al Pesto is a fine example of how delicious fresh pasta can taste. When owner Arlindo Campello saw us all reaching around the table, trying to share, he happily brought out extra plates and congratulated us for eating "family style, like the Italians do!" Thankfully, I saved room for dessert, and now I'm hooked on Basilico's Cannoli. The Italian pastry dessert must have been filled immediately before it was brought out to me, it was so crisp and the ricotta filling so light and creamy. Served with B&B coffee and donned with candied orange peel, it was, in a word, perfecto! *pr*

Explore

Places where the wide world is explained, nature abounds or adventure is to be had.

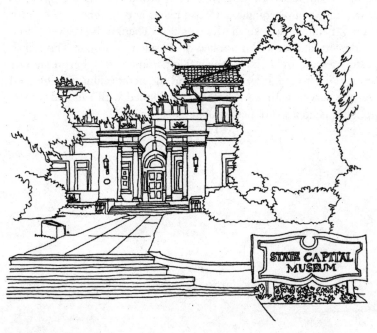

State Capitol Museum

Curiosity can lead down many a path; we've all seen our friend Curious George getting in over his head. But fostering a healthy curiosity about the world is as important as taking our very first steps. If we fill our imagination with programmed images and digital friends, we miss out on all there is to explore for ourselves in the big wide world. History and science, nature and adventure are waiting around the bend to expand your knowledge of the world around you. Seek out the big questions, ask your own, and most of all, enjoy the ride! *sb*

Washington State Capitol Museum

211 21st Avenue SW
753.2580
Open: W-Sa 11a-3p
Admission: $2

Maybe I'm biased because I love Washington, or maybe I'm just a sucker for museums, but this is a wonderful place to go and spend an afternoon learning about the history and culture of the Evergreen State. The museum is located in the historic Lord Mansion, and hosts a permanent collection of historic photographs of Olympia through the decades and artifacts from Western Washington's Salish Tribe. Their temporary exhibits are great too; last trip I was lucky to catch the exhibit showcasing woman's hat fashion through the centuries. *pr*

Japanese Garden

1010 Plum Street SE
Open: Everyday dawn to dusk
Admission: Free

Created in 1990 through the mutual efforts of the City of Olympia and sister City of Yashiro in Japan, the Yashiro Japanese Garden is an intricate sanctuary of time-honored garden designs. The fountains have a soothing effect on me as I wander the plush green landscape, finding places to sit while observing stone sculptures. A piece of me returns to Kyoto with visions of Ryoanji and Kinkakuji, once my neighborhood temples. I can even remember the exclamation for "cool" in Japanese: Kakkoii! *dm*

Hands On Children's Museum
106 11ᵗʰ Avenue SW at Capitol Way
965.0818, www.hocm.org
Open: M-F 10a-5p Sa 10a-5p Su 12-5p
Admission: $4.95-$7.95

This place is quite a treasure. The Hands On Children's Museum (HOCM) provides education through exploration and enjoyment. I used to nanny for a two-year old named Azura, and she literally *never* wanted to leave! If I told here it that *that* time, she would run over to the school bus on display and start madly honking the horn. The best part was, she could honk away and no one would sush her. This is a place for kids to be the free, wild beings things they are. Az also loved the art studio where she made a mess of total glitter, the building blocks (complete with a crane), and the "Tot Spot", an early learning gallery with picture books and tables full of lentils. HOCM also hosts birthday parties and puts on summer learning programs. After you tire of the museum, and succeed in dragging your kid out of the place, walk across the street to the Capitol Campus for a calming stroll. *pr*

Tumwater Historical Park
200 N Deschutes Way
943.2550
Open: Everyday, dawn to dusk

My friend Matthew and I walked this half-mile loop last autumn, collecting red leaves from the brilliant Japanese maples. We crossed footbridges and admired the natural landscape as we followed the Deschutes River towards its rumbling waterfall. Peeking over the edge of the bridge, suspended directly above Tumwater Falls, we threw our tiny red treasures over the rail and watched the water tumble them in a caldron and spit them out down stream. They floated down to the old brewery, as we walked back up to the picnic area, glad to have participated in the natural beauty of this great park. *pr*

Monarch Contemporary Art Center & Sculpture Park

8431 Waldrick Road SE, between Old Highway 99 and Military Road
264.2408, www.scattercreek.com/~monarchpark/index.htm
Admission: Free

Off of the I-5, down a 10-mile stretch of beautiful country road, there's a secret to be discovered: Monarch Sculpture Park. A hyperbolized red high-wheel bicycle lets guests know that Monarch is close, hinting at the many interesting sculptures and oddities to come. There is no fee to enter the park, though donations are much appreciated. Once here, you may find you have the whole place to yourself, which will be a good thing when you wind your way to the Sound Garden, an array of interactive musical sculptures. Arranged under a canopy of trees, these "musical sculptures" are placed in a pattern reminiscent of an auditorium so you can stage your own compositions. Director Myrna Orsini has created not only a public outdoor museum, but a creative enclave that hosts rotating resident artists, workshops, weddings and performances. I just couldn't help up giggle in awe at Orsini's own piece, a spin on her favorite childhood pastime pick up sticks. *dm*

Olympia Watershed Park

Eastside Street SE
753.8380, www.ci.olympia.wa.us
Open: Everyday, dawn to dusk

Watersheds are areas of land that gather the rain that feeds into our streams, rivers and oceans. Protection of this land is incredibly important for the proliferation of the heath of the water, animals, plants and overall welfare of our ecosystem. The City of Olympia prioritizes protection of their watersheds. The Olympia Watershed Park came into being when the citizens of Olympia did not want see the forests of the area destroyed by development or the waterways suffer. This 150-acre park contains the old city waterworks, with 27 wells, as well as walking trails. The trailhead can be picked up off of Henderson Boulevard near I-5 at exit 105. *dm*

Lions Park
700 Wilson Street SE
Open: Everyday, dawn to dusk

People watch a casual summer tennis match from the surrounding picnic tables as I plop down in the grass with my brown paper bag lunch from Big Toms. Lions Park is the best place in Olympia to see the Eastside Neighborhood at play. Catch Frisbee, play kickball or baseball games, and check out the large playground with your kids. *pr*

Schmidt Mansion
330 Schmidt Place SW
943.6951
Hours vary
Admission: Free

If you've ever been to Newport, RI, then you've seen the imposing historical mansions, once residences to powerful families like the Rockafellers and Vanderbilts. I don't think these families would ever have set foot in a "mansion" like Schmidt, but this belies the impressive slice of Olympia history that can be told from these grounds. And told it is, in the ancient oral storytelling tradition by a man named Bob. On most days, Bob can be found working on various projects around the mansion as he has been for the past fifty years. With little prompting, Bob will share his experiences working for the Schmidt family, founders of the Olympia Brewing Company ("It's the water"), starting out as the chauffer and caretaker of Clara Schmidt and eventually becoming manager of the house grounds. Bob has been witness to the seemingly perpetual flux of the old Olympia Brewing Company (sadly bought by Miller and no longer what it used to be) and the Schmidt land. He offers a personal insight into the prominent role this staple Olympia business has played in the history of the town and the lives of the town residents. The Schmidt Mansion is listed on the National Register of Historic Places, but "teller-of-Olympia-tales" Bob is the real draw of 330 Schmidt Place. Time spent hearing his tales will quickly bring you up to speed on what Olympia is all about. *dm*

Evergreen Beach

2700 Evergreen Parkway NW
866.6000, www.evergreen.edu/about/explorethearea.htm
Trail maps: www.evergreen.edu/tour/trailmaps.htm

Follow the signs to student housing and park at the back of F-lot. The trail winds down through groves of huge maples and firs, over a creek and down further to the beach. Don't be surprised if you see a few nude sunbathers in the summer, and if you don't feel comfortable around the "nudity-patooties," walk a bit further down the beach (only half the beach is nude). If the tide is low, enjoy the flat shiny mud banks with their chorus of shooting clams and geoducks. I like looking over to facing the banks of Steamboat Island, on a quiet day you can hear people talking across the water. Evergreen students have made maps of the surrounding trails, which come in handy if you want to make it a longer adventure. *pr*

Crosby House Museum

703 Deschutes Way SW, Tumwater
943.9884
Open: Seasonal Hours, call for more information
Admission: Free

I like to watch old movies on my work breaks, which has resulted in a huge VHS collection acquired from various thrift stores and depots around the West Coast. A recent arrival was "The Bells of St. Mary's," now my top choice Bing Crosby movie, (co-starring with Ingrid Bergman didn't hurt either). This was such a discovery! A classic film highlighting the frustrations and perseverance required to triumph over opportunistic business people with low-brow ethics and only the single bottom line in mind. Go Bing! So, of course I was happy to find that his hometown was Olympia, and you can walk through his family home and gardens re-living the wonders of his talent. Now I feel even more excited about this super star, and I suggest, along with picking up that film, that you check out his old haunts as well. *sb*

Listen

Any auditory experience you can imagine, from concerts to theater—its all here.

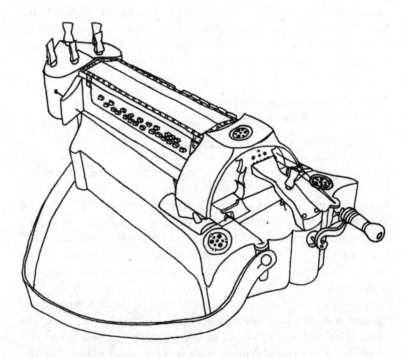

Hurdy Gurdy made by the Hackman's at Olympic Musical Instruments

Well-strung notes can carry every shade of human emotion. I like to close my eyes and let my other senses go when I catch wind of some magical melodies. My mother used to say you can't listen with your mouth open. But some of these places promote listening while you eat scrumptious meals and guzzle micro-brews. Olympia is a little city where music lovers and music makers abound. Whatever your ears perk up to, it is essential to enjoy the sounds and indulge in aural distraction as often as possible. *sb*

Kenneth J. Minnaert Center for the Arts
South Puget Sound Community College
2011 Mottman Road SW
596.5508, tickets: 596.5501, www.spscc.ctc.edu
This building houses two South Puget Sound Community College (SPSCC) theaters: Main Stage and Black Box. Both venues host performance groups from the community as well as in-school groups and productions including theater and music. Check the website or give a call to see what's on the docket this time of year. *dm*

Capitol Theater
206 5th Avenue SE at Plum Street SE
754.5378, www.olyfilm.org
The Capital Theater, home of the Olympia Film Society, also hosts a multitude of other cinematic, theatrical, and musical events. On Thursdays and Fridays local bands often play the Capitol Theater Backstage, which is accessed via a door in the alley. Donation is usually no more than a few dollars and the shows are almost always all-ages. Although it's quite a small space, the Backstage has an excellent sound system, so ear plugs might be a wise idea at electric shows. Nearly all local bands of any repute have played here, and famous acts of the past include The Gossip, Sleater-Kinney, Mirah, and many others. Few venues can claim to be closer to the hot beating heart of the Olympia music scene than the Backstage, and the friendly, intimate setting makes this an excellent place to go if you're interested in meeting the people who make the music happen. *jp*

Rec the Place Records

Inside Last Word Books
211 4th Avenue E at Washington Street SE
786.9673
Open: M-Th 11a-7p, F-Sa 12-7p, Su 12-6p

Don't leave Olympia without a quick stop into the back of Last Word Books, to the cave of records waiting to be discovered. The random selection will enhance any collection for a low price, whether you DJ on a regular basis, are learning how to scratch, or just like playing unique tunes while cooking up some grub like I do. Find a choral album from Alabama or a disco track, a jazz recording or a nice set of beats to lay down under layers of sound loops. Olympia musicians can often be found digging through the collections here. *sb*

Theater Artists Olympia

357.3471, www.olytheater.com
Various times and locations

A theater company that focuses on creative and experimental performances, Theater Artists does not shy away from the classics, but they will revamp them a bit, sometimes shockingly so. Check out TAO to see what provocative dish they have to serve up this month. Performances are held at area theaters, including the Kenneth J. Minnaert Center for the Arts. *dm*

China Clipper Club Café

402 4th Avenue E at Capitol Way SE
943.6300
Open: M-F 8a-2a, Sa 6p-2a, Su 2p-2a

With the DJ hiding up in a little crow's nest, the crowd boogying below and the bar line a bit too long, I step over to the 50's style booths for a water break. On a typical night at the China Clipper, the crowd is happily waiting for Scream Club, Olympia's electronic hip-hop band, to start their set. I've seen many great live shows here over the years, and with a fancy new mural showcasing local graffiti art, the Clipper is looking good. There's nothing much else to say except that if a band you want to see is playing at the Clipper, prepare yourself in advance for musty carpets and some rotten linoleum. *jp*

Independent Labels of Olympia

Any town with a thriving music scene eventually develops record labels to release the music to the wider public. Olympia has three: Kill Rock Stars, K Records, and YoYo Recordings. Kill Rock Stars, founded in 1991 by Slim Moon, is the largest and most successful of the three, and some of the more well-known musicians they've recorded include Bikini Kill, Bratmobile, Sleater-Kinney, Elliott Smith, and The Decemberists. K Records has been around since 1982, and is operated by Calvin Johnson of Beat Happening and Dub Narcotic. It has released music from the likes of Beck, Mirah, Modest Mouse, and Tender Forever. Yoyo Recordings is more informal and less commercial than the other two, and is best known for producing the Yoyo-a-Go-Go festival every few years. Yoyo has released music by Mirah, Nomy Lamm, and the Need. Sleater Kinney, a favorite of the GrassRoutes girls, also got their start on an Oly indie label, before rising to girl rock fame in the 90's. *jp*

Manium Warehouse

421 4th Avenue E at Jefferson Street

Amplified sounds and a youthful crowd of punky Olympians, Manium is known for its energetic dance scene and for being the only all-ages performance space around town. I attended their New Years Party one year, and I will never forget the rambunctious rockers thrashing around on the floor, then relaxing in the hot tub. When you tire of the music and dancing, take a drink from the Artesian Well, located behind Manium in the parking lot. *pr*

Washington Center for the Performing Arts

512 Washington Street SE
753.8585, www.washingtoncenter.org
Gallery Open: F 11a-2p

From Fall to Spring, the Washington Center is alive with Mariachi, stand-up comedy, classical concerts, dance performances and everything in between. Reasonably-priced season tickets will get you into the gallery and to many shows throughout the year. The Gallery has revolving shows where artists young and old, traditional and edgy fill up the space with their latest creations. Washington Center is the best place to see regional art, with natural light from well-designed skylights in all gallery rooms. Pick up a free brochure with the entire season's worth of shows and events. *sb*

The Brotherhood Lounge
119 Capitol Way N at Cherry Street NE
352.4153, www.thebrotherhoodlounge.com
Open: M-Su 4p-2a

The Brotherhood Lounge (also known as the BroHo) is one of the most all-purpose bars in town. A traditional haunt of Evergreen students ("greeners"), it's also a popular hangout with locals of all ages barring the under-18 group—it is a bar after all. Although it's not a gay bar, widespread dissatisfaction with the town's other gay bars has earned the Brotherhood a cynical reputation for being the gayest bar in Olympia. The beer is good, the cocktails are cheap, the shuffleboard table is well-oiled, and the covered patio in back gives nicotine-needers a place to smoke. The best time to go to the Brotherhood is when live music is being performed which, uniquely enough, is often on Monday nights. The Oly Rollers and the Tune Stranglers are regular guests, and both put on an excellent show. Local up-and-coming punk bands are often invited to perform as well. Don't despair, though, if you're not lucky enough to catch a live show the BroHo has one of the best jukeboxes you're ever likely to come face-to-face with. *jp*

Midnight Sun
113 Columbia Street NW at 4th Street N
705.4239

Of all the performance spaces in town, the Midnight Sun is the most unpredictable. You never know from day to day what eclectic performance you'll find there. This is due largely to the venue's practice of abstaining entirely from any creative control over the performances they host; they simply make the space available at extremely reasonable rates to whomever wants to use it. As a result it's not unusual for musical performances at the Midnight Sun to consist of stunningly bad bands self-producing their own shows. On the other hand, some of the finest musicians ever to reside in or pass through Olympia have played here. The Midnight Sun is an excellent venue to keep your eye on if you're interested in theater; many local productions showcasing the town's finest home-grown talent take place within, and stepping outside with the other audience members at intermission for a breath of fresh air, you're almost certain to experience the satisfying conviction that you're in the right place at the right time. *jp*

Rainy Day Records & Video

301 5th Avenue SE at Jefferson Street
357.4755
Open: M-Th 10a-8p, F-Sa 10a-9p, Su 12-6p

Undoubtedly the most complete selection of records and CDs in Olympia is found at Rainy Day Records. Locally owned and independently operated, Rainy Day will gladly special order any album that isn't already stocked in its overflowing racks. Music is certainly not the only thing on sale here; Rainy Day is also a video store with one of the largest selections of gay and lesbian films ever collected in one place, and a sizeable assortment of foreign films as well. You can also buy t-shirts, skateboards, Converse, postcards, zines, stickers, audio equipment, incense, and quite a bit more. This is an excellent place to lose track of time and wind up spending hours sifting through the colorful merchandise, previewing albums you're interested in, and searching the bargain bins and used records shelves for discounts. *jp*

Phantom City Records

302 4th Avenue E at Washington Street NE
705.3772, www.dumpstervalues.com
Open: M-Sa 11a-7, Su 11a-6p

Tiny, compact Phantom City Records, located in the same storefront as Dumpster Values, is certainly not the place to look for mainstream titles. Only a very careful selection of music is available here, consisting of indie rock and other music popular with the hip and jaded. The real niche this record store occupies is embodied in its selection of local and consignment records, where you'll find things that are available nowhere but here. Many of the albums in this section are homemade and self-released, some of them nothing more than burned CDs marked with permanent marker and stuffed in an envelope. Others are more elaborately assembled, and some of them are true works of art in handmade cases tied with silk thread or wooden latches such as you'd never find with more widely-released recordings. If you saw a local band play during your stay in Olympia but neglected to buy their CD at the show, then be certain to pay a visit to Phantom City Records before you leave town; it might not be available anywhere else! Phantom City is also a good place to promote your own music, or to pick up fliers for upcoming shows. *jp*

Evergreen State College Performing Arts
2700 Evergreen Parkway NW near Cooper Point Road
867.6000, www.evergreen.edu

The Communications ("Comm") Building at the Evergreen State College has several excellent performance spaces including the well-known Experimental Theater, and many noteworthy performances take place here. Evergreen's cross-disciplinary approach to the arts is evident in many of the performances, and it's not unusual for a single night to combine elements of music, dance, poetry, spoken-word, recorded media, and even lectures or seminars. Many of the performances that take place in the Comm Building are put on by Evergreen students, but plenty of other people use the space; dance and theater companies from out of town are often booked at the Experimental Theater. Oftentimes you'll see posters or fliers downtown for events taking place at Evergreen, but the best way to keep abreast of what's going on there is to visit the college campus itself (which is an experience worth having anyway), and read the fliers posted on the walls and bulletin boards all over campus. The Number 41 and 48 buses provide service to Evergreen, but the last bus leaves at 11p (830p on Sundays) so if you're thinking of attending an event that's likely to run late it's best to take a car or ride a bike. *jp*

Capital City Guitars
108 4th Avenue E
956.7097, www.capitalcityguitars.com

Located amidst the hubbub of 4th Avenue, Capital City Guitars is the repository for all things musical. Packed full of guitars and other instruments, they sell good high-end instruments and reasonably priced used equipment. You can even find locally made hurdy-gurdies there, a wooden instrument that makes a harmony of sounds by carefully spinning a wheel against three or more strings while keyboarding like an accordion. Be sure to check out the posters outside the shop for upcoming shows and house cafés that spring up to host various artists. Also known as secret cafes, these spots are a wonderful way to hear Olympia's best sounds and meet the locals, just ask around at City Guitar and you'll get the drift of what is currently planned. *pr/sb*

Arts Alliance Olympia

www.artsallianceolympia.org

Bringing the enrichment of the performing arts of Olympia's local community, the Arts Alliance works on behalf of the venues to grow awareness of the important cultural resources that abound. Art is what moves people on a deeper level, which in turn leads to positive growth and change. To that end, the organization works at the local level to raise awareness about the performing art's social, cultural and economic contributions through a collective voice. Subscribe to the AADO and you'll be front and center at the town's top concerts and theatrical performances, or make an impromptu visit to one of the theaters involved. Olympia's Symphony Orchestra and Masterworks Chorus are must-see musical ensembles in the area, and all their concert info is right on the Arts Alliance website. *sb*

Capital Playhouse

612 4th Avenue E
943.2744, www.capitalplayhouse.com

Located on the eastern fringes of downtown, the Captial Playhouse is the brainchild and magnum opus of the infamous Jeff Kingsbury, an influential local figure of considerable eminence. Plays and musicals held here are invariably well-produced and well-acted. Oftentimes local young actors star alongside professionals and companies brought in from out of the area. In the summertime the Capital Playhouse also serves as a rehearsal space for Kingsbury's Kids at Play program, involving area youth ages 8 to 18 in astonishingly well-produced musicals which are worth going to see even if you aren't personally acquainted with or related to a member of the company. The scope of these productions is vastly out of proportion to the capacity of the intimate Capital Playhouse, and the public performances are held elsewhere. Visit the box office for information on upcoming productions, or simply keep an eye out for fliers around town. *jp*

The State Theater

202 4th Avenue E
786.0151, www.harlequinproductions.org

The State Theater on 4th Avenue is the home of Harlequin Productions, Olympia's largest and poshest theater company. This is the place to come when you want to be seated in plush chairs, pay three dollars for a cookie and a cup of coffee at intermission, and take in a truly breathtaking performance. Plays at the State Theater are attended by more than just the elite, however; the first Wednesday of every production run is Pay-What-You-Can Night. Tickets for these performances are a scarce and coveted commodity, and you should be prepared to contest with jostling crowds and long lines at the box office, but it's well worth the effort. Where else can you put down two or three dollars to see a professional quality theater production? *jp*

Olympia's Little Theater

1925 Miller Avenue NE
786.9484, www.olympialittletheater.org

Olympia's Little Theater has been offering intimate live theater since 1939, and they have it down to a science. Producing classics like Cat on a Hot Tin Roof is challenging enough, but Olympia's Little Theater also produces original Northwest premieres and comedies. Everyone involved seems happy to be there, they serve free Batdorf & Bronson coffee before the show and hold up to their promise, "quality theater at a reasonable price." $10 tickets are available at buyolympia.com, or buy a five-ticket package for $40 and treat your friends to both a history lesson and a great live performance. *pr*

Get Inspired

Museums, installations, awe-inspiring exhibits and anything that aims to enthuse

Orca Books

The natural beauty and the scene at liberal Evergreen College continually rejuvenate Olympia's lively art community. Underground filmmakers and modern sculptors have found a steadfast community of equals here. With city-wide gallery crawls, and a strong commitment to sustainability and reuse in art, there are many straight-ahead creative minds converging in Olympia. Here is a listing of galleries, stages and museums that bring to the surface the artistic integrity of this part of the world. *sb*

Orca Books
509 4th Avenue E at Plum Street SE
352.0123, www.orcabooks.com
Open: M-Sa 10a-9p, Su 11a-6p

Oh the joy of a large independent bookstore! Literature was never meant to be as institutionalized as it often can be these days. Winding down stacks and stacks of titles at Orca Books makes me feel excited about learning more, and reading more often. The call of a Yeat's collection should never be denied and the thrill of a chronicle of the world's Ferris wheels is equally irresistible. Orca's got all their bases covered—there is even a 'Books on Books' section. This is a good place to chat it up with the staff for some suggestions to satisfy a personal library yearning and, if you're feeling musical, tickle the ivories of the piano by the curbside windows. *dm*

Childhood's End Gallery
222 4th Avenue E at Water Street
943.3724
Open: M-Sa 10a-6p, Su 1-5p

What first drew my through the entrance of Childhood's End Gallery was the beautiful mural of Japanese waves and boats on the side of their building. After browsing the fine art glass pieces in the gift store and the array of Pacific Northwest crafts, I entered the gallery space. I enjoyed a huge installation piece of neon underwater rocks featuring the most creative use of recycled soda bottles and Nerf footballs I have ever seen. Head to the back and you'll be surprised at the show in store for you. *pr*

Black Front Gallery
106 4th Avenue E at Capitol Way SE
786.6032, www.theblackfrontgallery.com
Open: Su-F 11a-7p, Sa 3-9p

Not only does Black Front provide a chic little venue for emerging artists, they also host events that promote community appreciation in creative ways. My favorite was the time when local authors were invited to re-create their desks as art-installations and have them read from their latest works. A non-profit gallery, it should be noted that the local artists love this gallery so much that many have donated works of art to the ongoing auction in hopes of keep the Black Front around. *pr*

Evergreen State College Art Gallery
2700 Evergreen Parkway off Cooper Point Road
867.5425, www.evergreen.edu
Open: Everyday, 9a-7p

Every time I'm on the Westside and feel the need to see fresh, oddly perfect, original works of art, I head to Evergreen State College and hit up their galleries. You know how some student artwork can be just a little too experimental? Or sometimes it's really pretentious and just painful to look at? You don't much have to worry about that here, the art reflects Evergreen's place as one of the nations top liberal arts-colleges. In addition to student art, they show regional masters and sponsor artist lectures. *pr*

Art House Designs
420 Franklin Street SE #B
943.3377
Open: Tu-F 10a-6p, Sa 10a-3p

A gallery as well as a music venue, I head to Art House Designs during the day to see local and regional work, and to admire the plethora of options at their custom frame shop. Nighttime at Art House is a different experience all together. One night I caught the last set of a full band, complete with an upright piano and cello. The most spacious yet intimate performance spot in town; Art House Designs is well equipped for the best of both worlds. *pr*

Last Word Books

211 4th Avenue E at Jefferson Street SE
786.9673, http://lastwordblog.blogspot.com
Open: M-Th 11a-7p, F-Sa 12-7p, Su 12-6p

When I first came to Olympia this was the bookstore where I first set foot, in search of another Steinbeck (I had just finished reading East of Eden as I drove to southern Cali and I was itching for more). I found far more than Steinbeck at this extraordinary bookstore. The somewhat haphazard categorization, with tags sticking out denoting sections like "Personality and Intellect," spills browsers into this bookstore's very own Zine library in the back (see the full review later in this chapter). Right inside the front door you'll find a good collection of pamphlets letting you know what's going on in a town where something exciting is always in the works. Last Word calls out "the man" on his evil workings and cries the battle charge for change; here you'll get inspired, get to reading and then get active. *dm*

Zine Library at Last Word

211 4th Avenue E, inside Last Word Books
786.9673, http://zinelibrary.net
Open: M-Th 11a-7p, F-Sa 12-7p, Su 12-6p

A zine is a hand-made, small issue, independent publication usually with an autobiographical emphasis. Because of their personal nature, zines are usually distributed through word-of mouth. Enter the Olympia Zine Library at Last Word Books and you'll be surrounded by an unofficial subdivision of Media Island. The shelves are stocked with zines of every flavor: fan-zines, political zines, comic zines and cooking zines. I like to grab a pile and tuck myself into the comfy reading nook. *pr*

Create

From beads to seeds, fabric to photos, these spots will enable your creative side for sure.

Bayside Quilting

I switched colleges my sophomore year to go to art school. I wanted to draw and paint and take photos all day instead of calculating chemical equations and studying political systems.

Later, I changed my mind and went back for international studies and English, but what I learned from the experience was something that hadn't crossed my mind before: everyone can create beauty; everyone can be an artist. I saw people who had never taken their pencil out of the lines on a steno pad draw impeccable contour figures by the end of one semester. Their eyes and their hands had become one unit. With a little drive, anyone can contribute to the beauty in the world. I also feel that it is important to maintain a connection with handwork. If you haven't ever tried something like this yourself, the satisfaction of eating something you have grown or cooked, wearing a dress you made, or a scarf you knit is astonishing. Your hands are the greatest machines. *sb*

Bayside Quilting
317 Capitol Way N and 225 State Street NE
357.2000, www.baysidequilting.com
Open: M-Sa 10a-6p
In two lofty downtown locations, Bayside Quilting brings up the chicken or the egg question for me. Did Olympia become such a great quilting community because of this great fabric wonderland or was it the other way around? Either way, Bayside supports an environment where people cherish quilts and strive to create these blankets of warmth and intricacy. Patterns for every mood and interest are wrapped around bolts in a range of hues—the music section has busts of Beethoven on flannel and music notes scattered across cream cotton, the flower section has yards of roses, hyacinths, daisy and daffodils ready to be covering your bed. The helpful staff doubles as quilt teachers, so you can ask them most any question on your journey for the perfect weave. *sb*

The Painted Plate
412 Washington Street SE at 4th Avenue E
705.2103
Open: M-Th 9a-9p, F-Sa 11a-11p, Su 12-6p
I used to think that painting a piece of factory issued pottery and then calling it my own was artistic heresy. But, after a few trips to the Painted Plate I changed my tune and was able to relax, sip a cappuccino and focus on the design aspect of pottery. The Painted Plate has tons of fun surfaces to paint other then plates: owl shaped piggy banks, tiny deer figurines and teapots. With anywhere from six to fifty dollars to spend, the young and the young at heart will enjoy painting the afternoon away. The Painted Plate also hosts painting-parties. *pr*

Colophon Book Art Supply
3611 Ryan Street, Lacey
459.2940, www.colophonbookarts.com
Colophon is known for quality bookbinding, paper marbling and Japanese *suminagashi* supplies. Interested customers are able to purchase these materials via mail order, but stopping by the retail shop is a unique experience you won't want to miss. Colophon is located on the most unassuming of residential streets in the tiny basement of a house, in true Olympia style. If you want to get into the craft of hand-bound books, Colophon is an inspiring shop to give you that needed jumpstart. Give a call ahead to make sure someone is home! *dm*

OPAS
1822 Harrison Avenue NW at Black Lake Boulevard W
943.6810, www.opasinc.com
Open: M-F 9a-6p, Sa 9a-5p, Su 11a-5p
When my student discount expired at OPAS it was a major disaster. OPAS is Olympia's one-stop art supply store and I'm there weekly buying pen-markers and pastels. Their paper selection is breathtaking: Italian gold embossed florals, thick banana paper, and all the standard weights for printmaking, bookmaking or sketching. The framing shop downstairs is standing by to put your next masterpiece behind glass. *pr*

Community Print

302 4th Avenue E at Washington Street SE, located inside Dumpster Values
Open: M-F 12-7p, Sunday workshops

Visiting a letterpress shop is one of my favorite pastimes. I revel in the nostalgia of this ancient craft, running my fingers over the indented papers. I stare in open-mouthed wonder whenever I meet someone who creates these works of art and fantasize that maybe I could work a letterpress myself someday. That day can now be any day I want. Community Print, tucked inside Dumpster Values, which, incidentally, shares a space with Phantom City Records, brings letterpress to all of us timid people with $15 tutorials and workshops for every skill level. An unofficial non-profit, this community organization also schools students in silk screening. Stop in to talk to someone or to find out the most recent contact info of who's in charge of scheduling as things tend to shift around. May my dreams and yours finally be realized! *dm*

Canvas Works

525 Columbia Street SW at 5th Avenue SW
352.4481, www.canvasworks.net
Open: M-F 10a-5p, Sa 10a- 4:30p

This vast store is wonderful for crafters and those with a list of projects swirling around in the back of their minds. You can come here to find rip-stop fabric or quality canvas to make a pack for your next hiking trip, get colorfully-striped canvas to re-cover your yard's sun umbrella or pick up balls of the softest mohair for some extra cuddly socks. The yarn selection features many local spinners, many of whom dye their yarn themselves without toxins. Rare wools and blends are available in many a range of textures, and thin threads are also stocked in force for more detailed work. The selection is incredible, and leads to a room full of knitting and crocheting patterns with a large worktable for classes and community knit gatherings. Don't miss the fabulous button collection, the beautiful dyed loose wool for felting or the laminated patterns that can be used like oil cloth as outdoor table coverings. Take your pick of wooden or recycled plastic needles, a treasure trove of findings, and tools for whatever your latest mission entails. *sb*

Shipwreck Beads

8560 Commerce Place Drive NE, Lacey
754.2323, www.shipwreckbeads.com
Open: M-Su 9a-6p

Touted as the biggest bead store in the world, there are more isles in this industrial-size space than at a membership bulk mart. You will start by winding through several unlikely business parks, but be reassured, you are going in the right direction. Right when you are about to turn around thinking you'll never find the Shipwreck you'll see a sign, small though it may be, pointing you to the right complex and onto the bead-encrusted sidewalk that will lead you inside. Once you're there you'll want to grab a rolling cart and peruse the rows of glass, semi-precious beads, and findings. The charm isle is the piéce de resistance—I spend an hour there and give the entire rest of the store about the same amount of time. Think of any action, talent, hobby or shape and you can find a metallic charm of it here; I got a campfire, a hot dog, and an antique sewing machine, all shiny and about the size of my fingernail on my last trip. The marvel of this epic store is the complete experience. Take a trip to the beading room, complete with TV, remote and tables for dozens of bead-happy crafters, and when hunger calls order a creamsicle milkshake from the better-than-expected restaurant located inside the store. No bead store tops this one. In the same location, you can purchase discount beads in massive quantities and have a cup of Yukon Chicken soup, made from scratch, all in the same location.

Scarlet Empress

109 5th Avenue SE at Washington Street SE
570.8800, www.scarlet-empress.com
Open: M-W 10a-6p, Th 10a-8:30p, F-Sa 10a-6p, Su 12-4p

Scarlet Empress draws me in. From the doorway, the wall of hundreds of rubber stamps is eye catching—it's enough to make me as giddy as a child. Papers, embossing kits, adhesives and ribbons fill the rest of this spacious store. Go online to shop, watch how-to videos and take workshops. Seldom you do you see a store so dedicated to crafting and scrap-booking. I use the treasures here to collage and make art and stationary, but you are sure to have you own inspirations. Don't forget to give Tinkerbell, the owner's sweet little Shih Tzu, a pat on the head before you leave. *sb*

Learn

Courses, classes, and seminars of all sorts, and places to take on new challenges.

Flexing your brain muscle is a great way to enhance a vacation, or a prolonged visit to a place. Classes are also a great way to meet locals. My grandmother was never bored; at the ripe old age of 82 she took Chinese language classes, having no background in it at all. She always inspired me to listen up, and see what I could learn. *sb*

Makeup Lessons at Premiere Salon and Spa
111 Market Street Northwest, Suite 101
753.3299
Open: Tu-Sa 9a-7p, Su 10a-4p
Who wants to admit that they need makeup lessons? Not me, but after years of avoiding the topic of makeup, I surrendered to the capable teachers at Premiere. The makeup lesson was painless, even for a Virgo like me, who hates to have her face poked at and brushed upon. I left with a feeling of confidence that my days looking like a goulish clown are behind me. The cost is twenty-five dollars and they ask for an hour of your time. *pr*

Media Island
816 Adams Street SE
352.8526, www.mediaisland.org
Open: Whenever the volunteer is there
As I approach the front porch of Media Island, I encounter three punky hippy kids who are heatedly discussing the hidden evils of free-trade. Media Island is a non-profit networking center, where people meet to discuss the crucial topics of social justice, economic democracy and peace. Their library showcases alternative books, CDs, zines, and videos specializing in first-hand sources of information. *pr*

The Tasting Room and B&B Roaster
200 Market Street NE across from Olympia Farmer's Market
753.4057, www.batdorf.com
Open: W-Su 9a-4p

Buy your coffee beans in the same building where they were roasted! The Batdorf & Bronson Tasting Room staff can answer all your coffee questions, and they are more then happy to brew a cup to "try before you buy," using the Clover, a single cup brewer that brings out the nuances of the bean. The first roastery in the US to be solar powered, B&B was green before it was cool to be green. Join the coffee pros at The Tasting Room for free cupping demos on the first Sunday of every month. The first time I attended a coffee cupping, I felt a little out of my league. All around, people sniffed at coffee grounds, making quizzical faces, saying things like, "A-ha! Lemon custard!", and when it came time to actually drink the coffee, they formed a chorus of quick slurping noises. But as Scott Merle (B&B's resident Roastmaster) explained the basics and answered questions about the various coffee regions, I relaxed and couldn't help but join in with their cupping-song. *pr*

Bayview School of Cooking
516 4th Avenue W near Water Street
754.1448, www.bayviewschoolofcooking.com
Class times vary

After a grocery shopping spree, or an ice cream cone on the go, grab a Bayview Calendar and get connected with to the most flavorful events and classes in town. From June to August, The Art of Fire and Smoke series gets you from novice to master barbecue chef. Each class has a unique focus like Greek-style barbecue or Baja Seafood. There's a book club that reads culinary mystery tales together, and epicurean trips to the region's top kitchens. Learn how to garnish, make Asian tapas, sharpen knives correctly or just get some solid wine basics. *sb*

Quilting Classes

317 Capitol Way N
357.2000, www.baysidequilting.com
Open: M-Sa 10a-6p, Su 10a-4p

At Bayside Quilting and their sister store, Bayside Quilting 2, there are spacious workspaces to learn machine quilting, from pattern cutting to piecing the top to binding the finished blanket. If you are interested in learning the traditional quilting techniques you can learn it from the friendly experts here. Try some organic cotton filer instead of the typical polyester for a warmer blanket, or bring in old clothes or fabric samples to be re-used as cuddly bedding. *sb*

Lengua Rica

303 10th Avenue SE
357.9924, www.lenguarica.org

When I was younger, I was flying to the US from Italy and there was a German boy, about my age, sitting next to me. He spoke German, English, Spanish, French and Italian and knew Latin as well. I spoke, well, English. United Statesians are not known for their lingual prowess, and I think that it is about time that we form a new reputation. Language is a path to culture and Spanish allows non-Spanish speakers access to Latin America, Spain and the many US immigrants who speak the language. Lengua Rica provides translation and interpretation services, but they also provide 8-week courses in the Spanish language, private classes and courses for children. After time spent with Lengua Rica, you might finally be able to watch the telenovelas on Telemundo. Ándale! *dm*

Waves Dance Studio

302 Columbia Street NW
705.9100, www.waves-studio.com
Class times vary

Line dancing, waltzing, even the Tango asks me to put aside my own unique movements and conform to a ridged set of pre-determined motions. Not so with Sweat Your Prayers! Sunday mornings at Waves Dance Studio finds me swirling around the room with 30+ other inspired people. Co-Owner Sara Pagano held the space for our discoveries while we thumped and bumped and cried and laughed. I did sweat, and I most certainly prayed. Also check out their 5Rhythems workshops, founded by dancer/philosopher extraordinaire Gabrielle Roth. *pr*

Music 6000

3738 Pacific Avenue SE
www.music6000.com
Open: M-F 10a-7p, Sa 10a-6p

When I stepped into Music 6000's new location the first thing that caught my eye was a shiny old accordion. The clerk practically jumped over the counter to play some polka, answering any questions I had before I could ask them. The selection is as great as the service; rows of guitars and bright pearl drum sets, new instruments and new ones line the walls of the store. I quickly found myself happily toying with two two-thousand dollar synthesizers and, thanks to the sound-proof sliding glass doors, making as much noise as I wanted. Music 6000 also offers piano, drum, and guitar lessons. *pr*

Get Active

Hikes, runs, rides, bikes, boats—anything and everything to get you moving

Olympia Skate Park

Whether you are simply getting from A to B, or seeking some good sweaty fun, getting active always has a refreshing result. I started on swim team at a young age, and have been known to go through various ski bum phases now and again. I've also been challenged by Pilates and yoga, and bouldering walls and rocks, indoors and out. Whatever thrill level you're seeking, from kayaking the sound to jogging Point Priest Park, Olympia is the kind place that offers all manner of sport and non-sport ways to jam. *sb*

Olympia Skate Park

Yauger Park, Cooper Point Road at Black Lake Boulevard
Parking in Capital Mall lot off Alta Street
Open: dawn to dusk

California Skate crew and park designers Purkiss Rose created this fun, but standard concrete skate park, where there's always a good group of folks trying out their skills. There's a 6-foot elevation from the highest to lowest points in the bowl, with a good mix of flat banks, ledges, and a snake run. The bowl is good for beginners, but you'll see pros from Bellevue, Tacoma and Seattle, all major skating cities pulling crazy handrail dogs on their way through town. Whether you skate or not, this place is fun to ride, or to picnic while you watch others strut their stuff. I like to come after a score at the grocery store-sized Thrift store across the street. *sb*

McLane Nature Trail

Delphi Road
Open: dawn until dusk

McLane Nature Trail is open year-round, and I like to go in autumn when the Roughskin Newts are mating. They tumble through the shallow sunlit water as duck families nibble grass from the floating logs. The shorter trail is wheelchair accessible, with boardwalks guiding us through the woods to the beaver pond. I have never glimpsed a beaver at McLane, but I have seen the lazy turtles sunning on the beaver dam. The longer trail is just over one mile, and has a neat bridge made from a fallen old-growth tree that balances over McLane Creek. *pr*

Evergreen State College Pool
2700 Evergreen Parkway
Pools are located in the CRC
867.6770, www.evergreen.edu
Open: M-F 8a-4:30p and 6-9p, Sa 10a-6p, Su 12-4p

I consider Evergreen State College's pool to be the only real pool in Olympia. They have your standard 25-yard by 25-meter lap pool: 11 lanes wide with a gradual slope from four-foot to 10-foot in depth. But what I really love is the 12-foot deep diving well! I did the math once and that well holds about a million gallons of water. If you time it just right, the pool will be all yours; one afternoon Mezzo and I practiced our pike dives, uninterrupted, for hours. Windows line the edge of the huge room, and the sun streaming into the pool sends dancing reflections up onto the high ceilings. After my swim, I go sit in the sauna until I'm cooked, and what's better then a sauna? *pr*

Steven's Field Park
2300 Washington Street SE

The all-American sport of baseball has always been true to my heart. It's the connective tissue of small town communities across the country for a good reason—its bundles of fun to play and to watch. Bring a crowd to play a game on one of their three diamonds, or cheer from the sidelines for one of the local leagues. Afterwards have a swing session on the adjoining playground. *sb*

Boat Rentals
312 73ʳᵈ Avenue NE
357.5670, www.bostonharbormarina.com

Drive towards the tip of one of Puget's fingers to Boston Harbor Marina, where boats bob in the surf, waiting for you to take the reigns. Kayaks are my vehicle of choice, being close to the water allows you to glide smoothly along the Pacific and gaze through the blue green at anemones in the shallows. Kayaks are $20 for two hours, just over $50 for 24 hours. Tandems are also available for a bit more. Canoes, pedal boats, and row boats are half the price, and fourteen-foot motor boats are $40 for two hours. The general store and gift shop atop the marina has a full pricing schedule and snacks for the road or water. After a midday paddle, pick up some local clams by looking for bubbles in the sand near the waves, or from the fridge on the dock for a reasonable price. *sb*

Priest Point Park
2600 East Bay Drive NE
www.ci.olympia.wa.us
This piece of Olympia land was first admired by missionaries who came to "teach" the Native American tribes their ways. In the 1840's Priest Point park was marked out as a trading, teaching and preaching post for Nisqually, Puyallup and Snoqualmie tribes, who were made to bring their boys to school at the mission. After the mission closed in 1860, the area was bought by environmentally-minded people who wished to preserve it rather than turn this prime location into housing or commerce sites. Now the park has Ellis Cove trail, one of the best jogs or walks in the city, a mini-cove off of the main Salt water bay with plenty of native plants and wildlife along the way. Bring a picnic and head to the Samarskind Rose Garden, or your puppy for a nature hike—you're sure to find beauty somewhere in this 314 acre bayside forest. *sb*

Vivala
3413 Capitol Boulevard SE at (one of two locations)
754.8482
Open: M-Sa 10a-5p
A small but complete source for athletic clothing and gear, Vivala promotes a healthy, active lifestyle and connects people with comfortable and functional garments. Sheebest and Horney Toad are both relatively local labels that make outfits that are breathable and moveable, without sucking resources dry. "Tread lightly" doesn't mean don't tread at all! *sb*

Pilates Center of Olympia
515 State Street NE
352.3444, www.pilatesatplay.com
Class times vary
Gymnastics gets a makeover at the Pilates Center of Olympia, where you can take invigorating Pole Dancing classes. One of the most fun ways to get fit, these music-filled classes get you swinging, swaying and sweating. For an equally physical challenge with more subtle movements, opt for a pilates class, taught by helpful and forgiving instructors who will help you get your muscles moved and your posture in check. Drop-in classes are around fifteen bucks, and a block of four classes is under $50. When you get a bundle of five Pole Dancing classes you only pay for four. *sb*

Briggs YMCA
1530 Yelm Highway SE
753.6576, www.briggscommunityymca.org
Open: M-F 5:30a-9p, Sa 8a-6p, Su 12-5p

Although I am sometimes tempted by the convenience of the downtown YMCA, it is worth traveling a bit out of town to get to Briggs YMCA. Located on the Intercity Transit bus line (route 15), Briggs YMCA is a newer facility, offering exercise rooms, a lap pool, and yoga classes. I like that the architects located the climbing rock next to the children's play-place, both are two stories high, and you can watch people of all ages play side by side through the glass. This is what community centers should be all about! Senior activities include swim aerobics, dance classes, and holiday performances. Briggs will let you tour the facilities before you pay, and their staff are always happy to assist you in choosing a class from the long list of offerings. *pr*

Black River Canoe Trips
273.6369
Various locations

Launching from Gate Road in Olympia, as well as from nearby Oakville and Rochester, these guided trips get you and your family onto and off of the waters safe and sound. In the spring and summer there is an array of purplish flowers at water's edge. The scenic view often includes the rocky Cascade mountain range in the background. Canoeing is a more relaxed exercise; you'll have fun to learning how to steer a boat with your oars. Take turns sun bathing in the middle of the canoe, just be careful to lather up in SPF so you don't get the ubiquitous life jacket tan. If you are quiet enough you'll see deer, herons and other wildlife enjoying the river with you. For experienced paddlers, you can rent boats from the same outfitter and launch in Littlerock, or have the boats toed to the location of your choosing. Consult with the experts at the rental office and their tips to guide you to a memorable tour of the Black River. Public fishing is allowed if you bring your own equipment or pick it up in town. *sb*

Olympia Yacht Club

201 Simmons Street NW
357.6767, www.olympiayachtclub.org
Class times vary·

The OYC has been around for about 100 years and has a great location near Bayview off of Percival's Landing. The club is private, with members who have moorage, event and activity privileges, but their classes are open to non-members. OYC Sailing School offers adult classes in the evenings, two days a week for two weeks. Check the website or give a call to see what the current schedule is. *dm*

Olympia Community Yoga

1009 4th Avenue E
753.0772, www.olyyoga.com
Class times vary

For over ten years Olympia Community Yoga has offered gentle and calming yoga sessions. With an emphasis on community development, Oly Yoga offers $6 yoga on the weekends. Because of the affordable price, community yoga has become just that, a studio packed with people of all ages, cozying up for the session. I enjoy arriving early, closing my eyes in meditation and listening as voices fill the room. When I open my eyes, "boom!" the room is full of people decked out in their funny yoga fashion. Classes are available everyday of the week, and beginners are always welcome. *pr*

Warehouse Rock Gym

315 Jefferson Street NE at Olympia Avenue
596.WALL, www.warehouserockgym.com
Open: Tu-Th 11a-11p, Sa 9a-9p, Su 11a-6p

Once you find it, don't be turned off by the unassuming façade and 'other side of the track' aura. The aptly named Warehouse Rock Gym plays daily host to area climbers of all abilities and levels of experience. Particularly during the winter months, when rain will chase even the most ardent of climbers indoors. Warehouse is a haven for those looking to stay in shape, hone their technique, or simply socialize with their fellow rock jocks and wall rats. With bouldering walls at 11 feet, and top rope and lead routes topping out at 30 feet, Warehouse offers a varied indoor environment to keep things interesting. *kt*

Hot Yoga Olympia

1963 4th Avenue E
956.9642, www.hotyogaolympia.com
Class times vary

Let's face it: Olympia winters are long, drawn-out affairs. The rain and the clouds...the gray ad infinitum. So imagine my joy when Hot Yoga Olympia opened its doors four years ago, offering ninety-minute classes in a room heated to 100+ degrees! Owners Margo and Anatol are the most committed yoga teachers I have met at any studio, their guidance allows me to surrender to the demanding series of 26 postures, and before I know it, the class is over. Knowing what grey dreariness awaits me in the parking lot, I am always the last one to leave, soaking in every ounce of warmth and wellness I can. Upon exiting, I feel relaxed, restored and calmly invigorated. *pr*

Olympia Mountaineers

www.olympiamountaineers.org

The Olympia branch of Mountaineers (not to be confused with buccaneers—those are pirates, silly!) is an incubator for the outdoor enthusiast. Skiing, hiking, climbing and kayaking are just some of the activities in which to participate. The Mountaineers also offer a range of classes from rock climbing to wilderness skills. Branch meeting are held quarterly at 222 N Columbia Street and their website is kept up-to-date with a list of the current adventurous undertakings. *dm*

South Sound Running

3409 Capitol Boulevard
709.2508, www.southsoundrunning.com
Open: M-F 10a-7p, Sa 10a-5p, Su 12-5p

Dedicated entirely to the sport of running, South Sound Running is a great resource for all those people who thrive on the rush of the run. From apparel and footwear to a knowledgeable and dedicated staff, this shop might just inspire the non-runner to start training for the next Lakefair Run (see **Calendar** chapter). There is also a section with information on area events and running groups, and the staff also know will fill you in on what's going on in the world of running. *dm*

Bike About

Oly Bikes
124 State Avenue NE
753.7525, www.olybikes.com
Open: M-F 11a-6p, Sa 11a-4p

A the corner of State and Washington streets, Oly Bikes is a landmark of local bicycle culture. Their employees happily demystify the numbers and measurements of my old 10-speed, and assure me that they can replace the blown-out tires even though they are practically antique. They also have a great selection of bike racks and lights for nighttime riding. Later that evening, I see my bike-tech zooming up the eastside hill on his Diamondback, and smile knowing my bike is in loving hands. *pr*

Western Chehalis Trail
Sleater-Kinney Road at Lilly Road

I like to get on the Western Chehalis trail at Sleater-Kinney Road, just past Lilly Road and ride up to Woodard Bay. The asphalt pathway makes for an easy ride, and this trail is well suited for dog-walkers, horse-riders and bicyclists alike. I pass a few couples with dogs, zooming past ponds and pastures. The farther north I go, the more the city breaks down into farms with chicken coups right next to the trail and old rusty equipment sculptures. When I arrive in Woodard Bay I am parched, but after circling the parking lot looking for water sources I realize I should have brought my own water. I turn and peddle home, glad for the easy ride back. *pr*

Grass Lake Trail
4599 14th Avenue NW

For someone expecting a nice easy walk to a wide glassy lake, I was quite surprised to find myself shooting through narrow winding trails, grass whipping my face and arms. Only later did I find out that the trail is for walking only, bikes are not technically allowed. The Grass Lake Trail leads to Olympia Grass Lake Refuge, touted as one of the best places for bird watching in the South Sound. *pr*

Bike & Bike
302 4th Avenue E
570.0608
Open: Su-M 12-4p, F 4-7p (ladies and trans only)
Located, like so many other organizations and shops, inside
Dumpster Values, Bike & Bike is a community instigator of bike
love. Here you will be able to build bikes, fix bikes, learn about
bikes and volunteer to help others do all this good stuff. The hours
are somewhat sporadic, so give a call or stop by to see if you can
use the space to attend to your two-wheeler today. *dm*

Olympic Outfitters/Bike Stand
407 4th Avenue E
943.1997, www.olympicoutfitters.com
Open: M-F 10a-8p, Sa 10a-6p, Su 11a-5p
A prime location for stocking up on outdoor gear while your bike
gets a groovy tune up, the Bike Stand has an efficient staff and a
great selection of utilitarian items for whatever type of trip on
which you are about to embark. The service is fast and while you
wait you can marvel at the ropes, active wear, carabineers and
helmets that are stacked around the place. Everyone around town
has made at least a few stops here to gather the necessary items for
their lifestyle—get a helmet fitting, a windbreaker or a super-duper
rainproof coat when it starts coming down in droves. *sb*

Re-Find

Take another look at what's been passed over, ahead is a treasure trove straight off a train from the past.

Olympia is a denizen of collectors. The long list of antique stores attests to that fact, and offers up plenty of opportunities for anyone with an eye for history. While away an afternoon chatting with an antique store clerk, and mulling over a record collection that ranges from 1940's to 1990's albums. At GrassRoutes we've taken the word re-use to heart, and applied it not only to re-purposing used yogurt containers, but to purchasing once-loved goods from thrift and antique stores, many in Olympia, our favorite city to shop. Rather than wonder if your new silverware set was made in China, get one that's made up of unique antique forks, knives and spoons. Use what we've already got circulating around the country rather than something brand new; if it is new to you it is just as exciting! *sb*

Thurston County Flea Market
Third weekend of each month, except July and December
3054 Carpenter Road, Lacey
459.1178
Open: Sa 9a-4p, Su 10a-4p
Nearly 50 antique dealers take over the Thurston County Fairgrounds one weekend a month so seekers can to bargain their way to material happiness. The large supply of linens and cloth make it an especially exciting array for the decorator and fashionista types, and if you don't yet have a sewing machine, you can find a well-made antique one at this mecca at another booth. Whatever your mission, be it purchasing Old World trinkets or just giving yourself some eye candy, you won't go home disappointed. *sb*

Inside Vintage
301 4th Avenue E at Jefferson Street SE
753.1520
Open: M 11a-6p, W-Sa 11a-6p, Su 12-5p
Inside Vintage keeps a small and selective collection of vintage threads. With a solid rack of jackets and a dazzling spread of dresses, this shop can outfit anyone looking for a bit of lost style. If you're lucky you might score an affordable cashmere sweater or an alluring 1940's nightgown. *dm*

Antiques Olympia
203 4th Avenue W at Water Street
786.9234
Open: M-Sa 10a-5p, Su 11a-4p
Showcasing a limited supply of the collectibles from different dealers, Antiques Olympia avoids the real low-budget pieces, opting instead for fine classic furniture, paintings and small corner curio figurines. They also provide a gratis map of the antique shops of Olympia at the door for those looking to make a day of it. *dm*

Harmony Market Antiques
113 Thurston Avenue NE
956.7072
Open: M-Sa 10:30a-5:30p, Su 11a-5p
I like to imagine the upstairs of Harmony's as my grandmother's closet filled with her flashy dresses and high heels from back when she was my age. In the corner there is a tiny dressing room where you can try on funky patterned suit coats and Levi's jeans. Browse the glass cases of Olympia Beer memorabilia including reissued buttons, stickers and mugs. My favorite is the belt buckle with a built-in bottle opener! *pr*

Courtyard Antique Mall
705 4th Avenue E
352.3864
Open: M-Su 10a-6p
This immense warehouse of re-finds will make anyone with even the slightest touch of the shopping bug giddy with excitement. With two floors of goods, the collection is an assortment of furniture, jewelry, old metal fence parts and other remarkable soon-to-be-yours home items. My favorite part of Courtyard Antiques is the bistro. Its black and white striped walls take me into a classic French café that couldn't be better suited to this mall of timeless pieces classics. *pr*

Dumpster Values

302 4th Avenue E at Washington Street S
705.3772, www.dumpstervalues.com
Open: M-Sa 11a-7p, Su 11a-6p

Filled with the warm, comforting, slightly musty aroma of second-hand clothing, Dumpster Values is one of Olympia's most dearly treasured fixtures. It could easily be argued that the town's unique fashion sense is born entirely within the four walls of this clothing shop, and certainly many of the people you're likely to see downtown will have assembled their outfits from the jumbled racks of miscellaneous clothing on display here. In keeping with its name, Dumpster Values eschews the vintage snobbery of many second-hand clothing shops, and offers its wares at extremely affordable prices. Be sure to do some rooting around in the dollar bin in the back, where any number of unexpected treasures can be found. The store will also buy any used clothing you're interested in getting rid of, and it's been speculated by some that Olympia's wardrobe is simply a fixed body of clothing passing back and forth between its citizens through the doors of this esteemed establishment. *jp*

Brown Derby Antique Mall

1001 Capitol Way S at Legion Way
352.8787
Open: W-F 10a-6p, Sa 10a-5p, Su 9a-3p

My mother had a row a tiny dishes lined up along the painting table in her studio, each with a unique and delicate pattern, some with gold leaf, and all with a different story of past journeys, friends or relatives. She'd sprinkle mineral powders in all hues into every one, and when the time came to brush with that color, the water she added would cover the small wells of each receptacle. As I walk through the many rows of colorful clutter at Brown Derby I am reminded of these precious paint plates and of the colors wrought from them, of time and the interweaving of family traditions and celebrations. From a family of creative types, I am naturally drawn towards collecting my own paint dishes, of which there are many here, undoubtedly used for something else in another household. This store is a collage of Washington life, with small price tags to bring a piece of it home to you. *sb*

Finders Keepers Antique Mall

501 4th Avenue E
943.6454
Open: M-Sa 10:30a-6:30p, Su 12-5p

We started collecting silver and silver plate silverware in mismatched pieces a couple years ago and are only about halfway to a full twelve-person service. After passing by a tempting lemonade jar, a rainbow of antique glassware, a pile of old records and a collection of black and white photographs, I found the star to our collection—silver pastry forks. With an almost knife edge on the far left prong, these hard-to-find utensils were incredibly inexpensive for their rareness. Bring your sharp eye, heaps of energy and motivation in order to get through this large mall of individual booths. There is an entire case of rhinestone jewelry, a wall-size one that is, and plenty of culinary tools that any home chef craves. *sb*

Centralia Square Antique Mall

201 Pearl Street S at Locust Street
736.6406
Open: Everyday, 10a-5p

Across from Washington Park, a brightly painted building towers the block. Head inside, and you'll be surrounded by shelves of goodies from the various phases and fads from America and beyond. Search for your own personal treasure on Centralia's three floors. Whether it's a large new-to-you vase, or a vintage outfit, after finding it you can gush to a friend at their in-store restaurant. *sb*

Buy Me

A unique take on shopping—from artichokes to zippers

The Tea Lady

Andy Warhol really was onto something when he equated department stores with museums. Indeed, the way to appeal to shoppers is an artful task, and well represents our most modern takes on design and cultural signing. So whether you have a practical purpose, need a little retail therapy, or just want to gaze at the most modern of museums, these spots should fulfill your aims, while also being community and environment-friendly businesses. *sb*

Tea Lady

430 Washington Street SE at 5th Avenue
786.0350, www.tea-lady.com
Open: M-F 10a-6p, Su 1-5p

Both ancient tradition and a respectable twist on domestication come into play on the fragrant shelves of the Tea Lady. Darjeeling, oolong, jasmine, and many, many more loose leaf and bagged varieties of global and local tea may be the primary reason to visit this inviting corner store, but certainly not the only appeal. What fun it is to explore the plethora of gadgets for tea steeping, the great variety of teapots, teakettles, French presses, and the imported edibles like British-born Hobnobs and McVitte's. Shopping at the Tea Lady gives the respect that is due to a modern domestic lifestyle—I find myself contemplating the purchase of a cute apron or some flour sack towels and relish household tasks. The Tea Lady is more than just a lovely place to purchase exotic teas and gifts for your friends; it also a small café where I like to sit down and enjoy a mug of Evening in Missoula (my favorite tea). Sit down to a comforting cup of your favorite leaf of tea accompanied by a satisfying slice of pumpkin bread. *pr*

Room 30
408 Washington Street SE
352.3300, www.rm30.com
Open: Tu-F 11a-6p, Sa 10a-6p

I swear Room 30 was teleported straight from the gift shop of some kitch culture museum. The jewelry case is home to some little colorful birds attached to graceful silver swoops, oddly shaped felt purses rest beside hand-printed stationary, and screen-printed cotton clothing is available for both men and women. Room 30 is a bit pricey, so keep in mind that spending locally is priceless (I have spent many a paycheck here). Owner Sara Rose searches the US for locally made treasures and smartly replies, "Everything is local to somewhere!" I love the children's section where I found little felt sushi and hotdogs. *pr*

www.buyolympia.com
Open: Anytime you can get a WiFi connection!

No matter where in the world you are, you can buy items made with love in Olympia. Set up in 1999 to help local artists sell their crafts online, Buy Olympia has branched out to include fabulous goods from all over. The site is nicely divided into sections like, "Things for Your Little Sister," and "Wicked Awesome Soaps." My favorites include: Stella Marrs' Olympia T-shirt (in honor of our long-closed Yardbird's Store), any purse by Queen Bee Creations, and Nikki McClure's yearly paper-cut calendar. You can also buy music from the best independent labels in town and buy tickets to local shows ahead of time (often at a discounted price!). *pr*

Compass Rose

416 Capitol Way S
236.0788
Open: M-Th 10a-6p, F-Sa 10a-8p, Su 11a-5p

A person without direction will find their way again with Compass Rose. This shop houses wares from around the globe, destined for your own abode or to spice up your next gift. The owner heads as far as Mexico for colorful wall art and as close as Seattle for jewelry like Faryn Davis' alluringly soft resin jewelry. Ditch Hallmark and jot down your well wishes on a card with an intricate x-acto knife design cut by local Nikki McClure (www.buyolympia.com). With your internal compass back on track, point to Batdorf & Bronson (see **Coffee Time** chapter), just a half a block away, for a post-shopping buzz. *dm*

Northwest Snowboards

2413 Harrison Avenue NW at Black Lake Boulevard
357.3727, www.nwsnowboards.com
Open: M-F 11a-7p, Sa 10a-6p, Su 12-5p

Northwest Snowboards covers the gamut of seasons. Of course snowboards in all sizes and designs are mountain-ready, but there are also surfboards awaiting waves,, skateboards itching for pavement and shoes just begging for some free-style walking. For great deals on styling jackets and other necessary apparel, head here in the off-season and negotiate an unbeatable price on the newest addition to your gear collection. NWS carries Olympia Lowlife screen-printed shirts, which beat out any cheesy souvenirs by a mile. This is the place to get stocked up for adventure and to find some chill people who share your love of riding. *dm*

Fireside Book Store

116 Legion Way SE at Capitol Way
352.4006
Open: M- Sa 10a-6p, Su 11a-4p

Pick a new volume from this friendly book nook and then choose between a café read next door or a spot in the park out front. Fireside has the best selection of hard cover photography books and local marvels like Olympia Walking Trails, the staff is helping and the selection of cook books will make you want to head right to the Farmer's Market or Bayview. *sb*

Sweet Life

528 Capitol Way S at 5th Avenue
352.7999
Open: M-Su 10a-6p

I don't know from experience, but I can imagine the role of a mother being a hard, albeit rewarding job. When mamas catch the shopping bug, needing respite from their 24-hour responsibilities, they can head to Sweet Life and find cute outfits and cuddlies for their precious one and also for themselves. As the mother of only a poodle puppy, I can still find sweet things at Sweet Life, like some adorable lingerie and perfect around-the-house clothes for those long days of writing in style and comfort. With a neighborhood feel and a feminine appeal, I like the frills and coziness of this centrally-located shop. *sb*

Bella Boutique

509 Washington Street SE at 5th Avenue
943.4335
Open: M-Sa 10a-6p, Su 12-4p

When your watch seems like a dull timepiece, your purse a utilitarian receptacle or your hands bare of bedazzlement, you know it is time to get glittered up at Bella Boutique. There is a pretty selection of rings and bracelets, many from local designers, and some cute handmade gifts. I brought my poodle with me last time I peeked in and he did a double take—they had a purse in the shape of a black poodle just like him! *sb*

Olympia Food Co-op

Westside: 921.Rogers Street, 754.7666, Open: M-Su 9a-8p
Eastside: 3111 Pacific Avenue, 856.3870, Open: M-Su 9a-9p
www.olympiafood.coop
CO or Check

The co-op holds a special place in the hearts of Olympians. With an endless supply of organic, local and non-GMO products, you can count on a real effort to promote sustainability and community. There's a deliberate selection of the items that are sold and a candid discussion of that process with its shoppers. The Olympia Co-op has established itself as a true breeding ground for ideas and actions that harvest a strong sentiment for conscientious living in the hearts and minds of locals. Beyond picking up your favorite foodstuffs, the co-op also holds events and classes, has a tasty salad bar, and is just a nice place to run into some friendly folks. *dm*

Mudbay Granary

2410 Harrison Avenue NW
352.4700, www.mudbay.us
Open: M-Sa 9a-9p, Su 10a-7p

Not only do the staff at Mudbay kindly answer my millions of questions about the raw-food diet my cats are on, they give me three different frozen patties for free! They also know all sorts of tricks, like using a cheese powder to keep kitty (and puppy) teeth clean, so as to avoid the torture of attempting to open the mouth of your feline. A wide array of cat and dog toys and cute collars and leashes, plus on-site grooming and doggy daycare, Mudbay Granary is the place to go for healthy dogs and cats! *pr*

Danger Room Comics

201 4th Avenue W at Capitol Way S
705.3050, www.dangerroomcomics.com
Open: M-F 11a-8p, Sa 11a-6p, Su 1-5p

It's a bit nerdy, but I'll admit it: I had a comic file at Danger Room
Comics. Whenever the latest Dame Darcy or Julie Doucet comics
were released, they would be routed directly into my file. The
helpful and charming staff answered my questions and guided my
interests toward the alternative comic authors I have since grown
to love. One manager even picked me up a rare Megan Kelso
comic at a convention in New York and brought it home to my
file! I love the local zine section, full of autobiographical comics
and prose by Olympia's budding authors. Grab a comic and hang
out a while. The Danger Room hosts events all year round, my
favorites include free-comic book day and their Comics Festival,
find it in the **Calendar** chapter. *pr*

Hot Toddy

410 Capitol Way S
753.0868
Open: M-Sa 10a-6p, Su 10a-5p

Scene: Parlor-room music is playing from Olympia's KLADY am
radio station, and owner Sydney Hann is sifting through small piles
of gold, silver and plastic. We are in Hot Toddy, a store-sized
explosion of Sydney's wicked-fancy sense of style. Instead of
abandoning Olympia for some brighter scene, she chose to stay
and help elevate us. Sydney goes to Brooklyn every year for their
huge craft fair and brings home a wealth of accessories: cute
picture rings and bracelets and really femmy pocket-watches. From
the racks of dresses in every shape and size, (some made locally) I
select a little chartreuse 50's number and slip into the curtain
tangles of the dressing room for a bit of dress-up. Of course it fits
just right, and I'm out sixty bucks. The children's clothing section
offers a wide selection of unique items to get your girls looking like
hip little queens! *pr*

Bayview Thriftway
516 West 4th Avenue at Budd Inlet
352.4897, www.bayviewthriftway.com
Open: M-Su 6a-12a

This locally owned grocer has arguably one of the best locations in town. After a morning jaunt down the lovely Budd Inlet boardwalk, Bayview is a handy stop for your grocery needs. Aesthetically pleasing décor and a most helpful and gracious staff make Bayview feel like a second home. Their bulk section ain't too shabby either. I like to pick up some candied ginger in bulk and nibble happily as I head out for a day's wanderings. The umbrella company, Storman's Inc., owns a couple of franchises of chain businesses, but their two Thriftway stores (there is also Ralph's further down 4th Avenue to the east) are staples of the Olympia community, providing employment and provisions for residents and visitors alike. Electric car plug-ins are available in the parking lot. We all love their deli so much, there's more about it in the **Do Lunch** chapter. *pr*

Wind Up Here!
121 5th Avenue SE at Washington Street
352.1228, www.winduphere.com
Open: M-Sa 10a-6p, Su 11a-5p

When I was a kid there were few temptations greater than mini animal figures. Now you'll find my collection hot-glued to the entranceway of GrassRoutes headquarters, lined up giraffes and dinosaurs marching every which way. If I were a child again I would be just as glued to Wind Up Here!, where bins of lizards, frogs and pigs are lined along the back wall, waiting for you to stick your hand in and find the right one. Check out the large finger puppet collection, and the hysterical costumes and masks. I appreciate the focus on natural toys rather than plastic fads—they go in and out of fashion with over-stimulating games that sap out a child's innate creativity. Instead you'll find things that will be passed down and shared with several generations. *sb*

Sunny Tree Market
131 Decatur Street NW
943.9633, www.newvege.com
Open: M-F 10:30a-8p, Sa-Su 11a-5p

Sunny Tree combines the two food grocers that I enjoy going to the most: Asian food markets and natural products grocers. Here I find udon noodles, Hoisin sauce and mochi ice cream balls alongside fair trade teas, rice milk and organic energy bars. The atmosphere is pleasant, with beautiful wood shelving and friendly owners. One of the highlights is the juice bar connected to the grocery section. An array of milk teas and juices come in flavors from coconut to avocado, with mostly organic ingredients and the option of tapioca balls at the bottom. Sunny Tree is an oasis, an escape from busy Harrison Avenue and the *zabuton* cushions by the window provide a wonderful sense of an Eastern way of living in Western Olympia. *dm*

De Colores Books
507 Washington Street SE at 5th Avenue
357.9400, www.decoloresbooks.com
Open: M-Sa 10a-6p, Su 10a-5p

De Colores is a great resource of books specializing in multicultural awareness. They have bilingual children's books that teach about immigration rights and language learning. I like the spirituality section, which offers non-denominational guides to self-discovery. They also have lots of used books in other languages, from French travel guides to African novels. *pr*

Archibald Sisters
406 Capitol Way S
943.2707, www.archibaldsisters.com
Open: M-F 10a-7p, Sa 10a-6p, Su 11a-5p

Going beyond the typical cheesy gag gifts and sex toys, Archibald Sisters follows in this vein in a much more palpable and pleasant way. This shop is chocked full of things crowd pleasers and unique party favors. Beyond these exciting options for entertainment, Archibald's formulates over 100 of their own fragrances, the most popular ones being Oly Girl and Oly Rain. A visit to this store could be an outing in and of itself, with much more interactive fun than a trip to the movies. *dm*

Sol De Mexico

2413 Harrison Avenue NW at Black Lake Boulevard SW
753.2342
Open: M-Su 9a-9p

My parents made it a ritual to go to Mexico every couple weeks. OK, not all the way south of the boarder, but we would find the authentic Mexican restaurants all over New York, New Jersey and Pennsylvania when I was young. It wasn't until later, when I wasn't in the habit of eating at many restaurants, but instead trying to recreate my favorite dishes on a budget, that I tried replicating some of the tasty traditions of Mexico. With Sol De Mexico right around the corner, I have everyday access to the key ingredients: chocolate mole, handmade tortillas, green chiles, hot peppers, hominy, fresh cheese and of course beans of plenty. Now I have gotten decent at fresh veggie-filled tostadas where I shape large soft tortillas into crispy shells, and even chile rellenos, where battered and stuffed peppers get doused in fresh tomato sauce. Try your hand at creating a new edible masterpiece! *sb*

Capitol Market

2419 Harrison Avenue NW at Black Lake Boulevard SW
956.7124
Open: M-Su 9a-8p

Find Vietnamese snacks, tummy-pleasing pho soup and a fully-stocked market of traditional Asian ingredients at the best market of its kind in town. In the fridge cabinet, look for the plastic cups of strange-looking pudding, but don't be weirded-out by the interesting shapes and colors caught between mung beans and tapioca pearls. The thick one with a white layer on top is banana tapioca pudding with fresh coconut milk, and by far my a favorite choice. I also like the more liquid dessert with different beans and sweetened seaweed inside—it is delicious despite how the ingredient combination may sound. Along the vegetable isle look for fresh lychees when they are in season, or crispy lotus root that is sublime sautéed with sesame oil, soy sauce, carrots and burdock root (be careful to peel it well). Cans of surprisingly good veggie curry make this the spot for last minute, lazy late-night grub. I stock up for a few days at a time when life gets especially busy, that way I only have minimal microwaving and stirring to do rather than getting carried away by another one of my involved cooking projects. *sb*

Farm to Table

Agritourism is at its height with this selection of farms, u-picks and glorious garden stands.

Olympia Farmers Market

Connecting with the source of your food is a wonderful step towards sustainable living. How can you look at produce or a list of ingredients the same way after having the experience of talking with your local berry farmer or seeing an egg being hatched? Somehow we got sidetracked and chemicals slipped their way into our foods, but we can think a little bit before chomping down and make sure we are as natural as the living beings we are. Escape to the countryside and reconnect with the importance of beautiful, bountiful food. *sb*

Olympia Farmers Market
700 Capitol Way N
352.9096, www.olympiafarmersmarket.com
Open: April-Sept Th-Su 10a-3p, Nov-Dec Sa-Su 10a-3p
Organic produce, fresh fish and shellfish, eggs and cheeses, jams and sweet pastries; Olympia Farmers Market has it all. A balloon man covered with his own creations constructs balloon poodles and dinosaurs while families eating curry, bratwurst, crab cakes and Mexican food circle around the covered stage listening to musicians sing out. All the while an illusive cinnamon fragrance will lead you toward Jawa gourmet roasted nuts, where I happily sample and buy the lime-in-the-coconut almonds. After my market experience, I like to go walk to Percival Landing to skip rocks while grazing on my bountiful purchases, which include ready-to-roast asparagus, fresh bread and smoked cheeses. *pr*

www.pickyourown.com/WAsouthwest
This amazing resource directs the argi-tourist to edible goldmines all over the US and Canada. Go to this area of the site for the local bounties of western Washington, where there is an incredible array of farms and u-pick options. Get up close and personal with the farm and get recipe recommendations on the site too. One of the best ways to travel is to explore the local agriculture, so try it out for yourself. *sb*

Perennial Gardener

5424 Boston Harbor Road NE at 53rd Way NE
754.8084
Open: Th-Su 10a-6p

To start a garden up, or keep one going, all the supplies and plants can be found at the Perennial Gardener. An exceptional selection of geraniums and elegant hanging baskets can spruce up the porch or window boxes of the friend whose sofa you are crashing on (I always like to gift come with something pretty in hand for to my gracious hosts). For keeping up a garden amid the varying temperatures of Puget Sound, you'll get all your questions answered, and after you figure out where to get started, you can take your planning conversation to the Boston Harbor Marina for a chowder snack and a good talk about which spot in your yard to start with. *sb*

Thurston County Farm Map

www.fertileground.org/foodshed

At most coffee shops, or the reading stacks at many local eateries, you can pick up a free map of the nearby farms and farm stands. This resource will get you to the pastures, fields, rows, sheds, barns and haystacks of the farms of the county. Whether you have a hankering for fresh-pressed cider or just want to pick your own bouquet of organically grown flowers, take a good long look at this free map and info guide before you head to the farms. It's also all online! *sb*

Helsing Junction Farm

12013 Independence Road, Rochester
273.2033, www.helsingfarmcsa.com

A nearby, certified organic farm, Helsing Junction signs on members to their CSA (community supported agriculture) for regular pickups or delivery of a variety of fruits and vegetables. The shallots, squashes, sage and more from these plots of earth will liven your meals in a tasty and healthy way. If you are staying a while, join up and get a pile of veggies for about thirty dollars a week, or just come for a visit and a stroll along the rows of Dr. Suess-esque Brussels sprouts. *sb*

U-Pick Blueberries

Black River Blues Blueberry Farm, 17132 Moon Road SW, Rochester, 273.3489
Carr's Organic Blueberry Farm, 3844 Gull Harbor Road NE, 352.3739
Fischers Blueberries, 31002 Friendly Grove Road NE

Olympia has the perfect weather for chubby blueberries, packed with flavor and sweetness. There are three farms where you can pick your own from these thorn-less bushes. Look under the branches toward the lower leaves for the berries others miss and you are sure to find a gold mine. Black River Blues Blueberry Farm has a bountiful crop of 17 varieties in July and August, and is open everyday except Sunday from 10a-6p. They also have honeycomb you can chew on while you pick or save for a sweet treat afterwards—my favorite! Carr's Organic Blueberry Farm is, as the name states, organic, so sweetness is multiplied here. Pick everyday from 9a until dusk. Fischers Blueberries are grown in a beautiful, rolling hill landscape in Olympia, and has a later crop from August to Septmember. Although they aren't certified organic, they use no pesticides on these berries, so come out Tu-Sat 9a until dusk. It's the farm where Boston Harbor gets the berries for their amazing pies. *sb*

Lattin's Country Cider Mill

9402 Rich Road SE
491.7328

East, west and, er, north have been covered, so it's about time to head to South Olympia and see what's going on in that neck of the town. Bring the chilluns to Lattin's anytime of the year and their faces are sure to light up with innocent glee. Pigs, goats, ducks, rabbits and a peacock are just some of the animals ready for attention and, possibly, some feed purchased inside the Lattin's store. There is also Lattin's own apple butter, pickles and jam for your own pleasure, for the folks back home or for your gracious Olympia hosts. This seasonal spot puts on all the necessary calendar events like Easter egg hunts, an Applefest, pumpkin patch picking and, of course, Thanksgiving pie sales. *dm*

Left Foot Organics
11122 Case Road, Building L
754.1849, www.leftfootorganics.org
In an effort to provide healthy and happy employment for community members with developmental disabilities, Left Foot Organics emerged. LFO is a non-profit garden, with developmentally disabled growers cultivating produce that is distributed to local markets like Olympia Co-op (see **Buy Me** chapter), as well as town residents, through their Community Supported Agriculture (CSA) shares. There are numerous volunteer opportunities available and the goods can also be picked up at their farm stand south of Olympia, F 2-6p and Sat 10a-1p. *dm*

Steamboat Island Goat Farm
9201 Steamboat Island Road NW
866.8568
Steamboat Island's naturally grown, grass fed goats supply Oly with milk and cheese alike. This farm opts for raw milk, which means that though it is naturally homogenized it has not been pasteurized and so has active enzymes and flora. Goat's milk and cheese are easier for lactose-intolerant people to digest, and they are mighty tasty! I like to go to the farm to give the goats a pat on the brow! *sb/dm*

Schilter Family Farm
141 Nisqually Cutoff Road SE
459.4023, www.schilterfamilyfarm.com
Open: Seasonal hours, open daily
To the far east of town, is Schilter Family Farm, fun for the whole gaggle. Their farm market is open year round to pick up some fresh fixings. There are seasonal happenings like selecting your pumpkin from the patch and navigating the ever-evolving corn maze (one year it was a map of the US). *dm*

Chehalis Farmers Market
Boisfort Square, Chehalis
880.9546
Tuesday, from noon to 4p at the Boisfort Square, the Chehalis Farmers Market comes alive with fruit, vegetables and a strong community feel. This market is the best place to find jams made from berries that love growing plump and juicy in the regional climate. *dm*

Lacey Farmers Market

Huntamer Park, 7th Avenue at College Street
491.3214, www.ci.lacey.wa.us
Open: Sa-Su 10a-3p

Throughout the summer months local musicians will strum away while you admire very recently harvested produce and craft tables. Living in the shadow of the popular Olympia Farmers Market isn't easy, but this new park incarnation gives the Lacey market an air all its own. I like coming here with no particular purpose other than to buy enough to make a complete meal. Base your next feast on what is in season here! *sb*

Calliope Farm

1335 Overhulse Road
866.4257

Not only is Calliope the muse of epic poetry, but she is also a farm located close to downtown Olympia. Calliope has begun to sell at the Farmer's Market and also offers CSA subscriptions. Their produce is chemical-free, and although they do grow their veggies and herbs without pesticides organically, they haven't paid "the man" for an official certification. Maybe the current divine form of Calliope is the muse of organic farming. *dm*

City for Free

The ultimate guide to free events, free admission, free talks and more

Old Capitol Building

Just as the saying goes, "the best things in life are free," we've searched high and low to find the best free things in Olympia. These great events are all adventures that don't involve digging into your wallet. Don't forget that hiking and enjoying a city walk are also great free fun. *sb*

Old Capitol Building
On Boundary Street SE, bordered by Legion Way, Eastside Street and 8th Avenue

You can't have a visit to Olympia without a good long hangout in a grassy park. That just wouldn't do at all. After a trip to Wind Up Here! Toys (find it in the Buy Me chapter), with Frisbee in hand and flanked with friends, the old Capitol building is the backdrop for hours of silliness and delightfully low-key fun. Sit on a bench under some grandfather trees and marvel at days gone by. It isn't a big park but it is centrally located, which makes it a convenient place for all that "hanging" you are about to do. *sb*

Legislature and Supreme Court Viewing
416 Sid Snyder Avenue SW
586.3460, www.ga.wa.gov/visitor
Session times vary, but are all during business hours on weekdays

When in session, bearing witness to the proceedings of the Washington Legislature and Supreme Court gives citizens a chance to see democracy in action. The sessions of the Legislature vary from year to year, but begin in January and end in the spring. Supreme Court hearings, when they happen, provide insight into all those court shows on TV these days. If there are no happenings on the day you stop by, no matter, these edifices are a marvel to behold; the cupola of the Justice Building is grand and the Law Library of the Temple of Justice is a hideaway of solitude, with tables at which to read or gaze at Capitol Lake. *dm*

Artesian Well Drinking Fountain
4th Avenue between Jefferson and Adams Streets
Open: Anytime you are thirsty

Washington State and Thurston County are working with Friends of the Artesians to establish a park area for Olympia's aqueduct, but for now the Artesian Well is a pipe sticking out of the cement in a Diamond pay-parking lot. That doesn't sound very welcoming, but recently people have added some painted brick squares to sit on and a few planter-boxes full of flowers, making the Artesian Well a more comfortable place to relax and fill your water bottles. Legend has it that once you have tasted the water you will be destined to return to Olympia, so drink up! *pr*

Timberland Regional Library
313 8th Avenue SE
352.0595, www.trlib.org
Open: M-Tu 10a-9p, W-Th 11a-9p, F-Sa 10a-5p, Su 1-5p

When I was a little girl, a trip to the library was quite an expedition. If I was lucky I could tag along with my dad to the gigantic Free Library of Philadelphia library where he'd pick through their huge collection of classical sheet music while I dove into the fiction section. Miraculously, Olympia's rather complete selection fits into an unassuming tawny brick one-story, where people pile in and file out with a stack of books in the crooks of their arms. In Olympia the plethora of avid readers and concerned citizens make regular trips to the library. Their up-to-date system is easy to use and, as is the norm in Oly, the librarians exude friendliness. *sb*

Olympia Free School
610 Columbia Street
www.olympiafreeschool.org
Class times vary

I was raised on the saying, "I learn something new everyday." My mother used to chime in about all the things we could learn and showed me that the classroom wasn't the only place to do it. When you are in Olympia, the general vibe is of trading skills and smiles, and OFS is the place where it all comes together. Take a Chinese language course or learn how to harvest potatoes. Get involved in a community potluck where new class ideas are being birthed. The locations vary but all the info is online; fall and spring there are the most populous scheduled events. *sb*

Olympia Coffee Roasting Company Cuppings
203A 4th Avenue
352.4628, www.olympiacoffeeroasting.com
Open: Call to request a cupping

There are coffee blends from around the globe and Olympia Coffee Roasting Company will give willing participants a taste of some select brews in their downtown cupping room. Cuppings, as they are called, are available upon request, so give them a call to see when you might be able to delve into the gourmet world of the coffee bean, a mandatory Oly pastime. *dm*

Samarkind Rose Garden
2222 East Bay Drive in Priest Point Park
753.8380
Open: dawn to dusk

Along the East Bay, you can walk by bobbling ships and watch as the stately Capitol Building and masses of evergreens peak through the clouds. Take a little more time and jog through the single strip of houses along the shore, collectively the East Bay neighborhood, and into Priest Point Park. At the main entrance, where various jogging and hiking trailheads converge, you'll be enveloped by fragrant roses of all hues. Each bed is mélange of plants, some that are used to attract aphids away from the roses so that no pesticides need be used to keep the garden happily blooming. Sit with a book under the clematis-covered arch and you'll be in the quintessential Olympian paradise. *sb*

Waterfront Public Art Tours
Percival Landing, beginning at the bell in front of the Farmers Market
709.2678, www.ci.olympia.wa.us/cityservices/par/

Self-guided or guided (call the telephone number to schedule a tour), navigating the large collection of public art in Olympia is a pleasant way to take a walk and take in some culture. Pieces are scattered throughout the city and many have phone numbers to call for a description of the artwork. I can't imagine a world without artists and their fine creations; their contribution to culture is priceless. Luckily viewing public works comes without a price tag. *dm*

Loitering

When I first arrived in Oly, the town was covered with a fine of mist and a darkened sky. Granted, it was a Sunday and many businesses and workers had the day off, but the number of people just lounging about outside under the overhangs of the downtown establishments with no apparent responsibilities or obligations was astounding. It took me a while to grow at ease with the slow pace of Olympia, but I recommend that you let it get under your skin, in the best sense of the term, and settle into the speed. Though there are definitely the proverbial wackos who floating around, there are also those interesting folks who will strike up an hour-long conversation with you at the drop of a hat. If you are open and willing you can feel like a local in no time, but if you don't feel like interacting, pass some time people watching and get started on understanding what the unique vibe of Olympia is all about. I'm still not quite sure how they all bring home the bacon, but I like their style. *dm*

Pamper

Shelters from the hustle and bustle, simple enjoyments, and all things feel-good

Desserts by Tasha Nicole

Part of the whole pampering process is good, hot, comfort food. The classic is chicken soup. But I find most places load their chicken broth with salt, as a substitute for slow-cooked flavor. This is bad news for the body; instead of pampering you get seriously dehydrated. So, in this chapter I've given special attention to not only the in-the-moment effects, but the after effects as well. Here is a selection of feel-good foods, restful spaces, and of course, spas and salons to refresh, re-energize, and restart your engines. *sb*

Desserts by Tasha Nicole

2822 Capitol Boulevard S
352.3717, www.tashanicole.com
Open: M-Sa 8a-5p

On a back counter of the circular bakery are stacks of foreign catalogues and order forms. Most of them are in two or three languages, so the bakers learn the words for the best chocolate in the world, or the finest rose extract, or the most marvelous Danish marzipan in order to collect these special ingredients for their pies and cakes. The top dollar prices for rose cream cake, German chocolate or tropical cake, made with pineapple liqueur, are directly related to the bakers casting their nets wide and far to find the finest and freshest ingredients from around the world. Once their pantry is stocked, cakes of all shapes, sizes and flavor combinations are dreamed up, baked up, and served to you. Even though you can find their desserts at a few top restaurants and stores around the area, I like coming into their lace-curtained store for a slice of the day and a cup of free trade coffee with lots of milk. *sb*

Boston Harbor Pies

513 Capitol Way S at Legion Way
705.3180
Open: Tu-Sa 10a-5:30p

On the main drag of downtown there is a small storefront, stucco-ed in algae-color paint with a quaint (dare I utter that word?!) sign and archway. Please take the time and follow your nose, and the signs beckoning you towards chicken pot pie. Boston Harbor Pies are the time-honored creations of a local woman who can out-do all the rest with her sublime cherry pie. I would drive over hill and dale to get a slice of it, stuffed with real sour cherries and filled with just the right balance of crust to fruit. No fillers or preservatives, just the flakiest crust and the perfect tartness becomes this epic slice of pie. If there are samples on the counter, and there usually are, try one, but I can't stray from the cherry myself. For lunch take a chicken pot pie home with you, or order a banana crème pie to go, they are awesome but only made to order. *sb*

Capital City Flowers

515 Capitol Way S at Legion Way
357.5757
Open: M-F 9a-6p Sa 10a-4p

May Sarton wrote that without flowers she would die. It's a bit dramatic, but I agree. Whenever I need a single stem for myself, or a bouquet for my mom, I head over to Capitol City Flowers. The glass cases are eloquently stocked with the finest, and owner Cynthia Salazar is usually working on some exquisite living sculpture, a special order for a wedding or anniversary. They also offer a weekly floral subscription, which is really the best gift-idea I have ever heard of, ever. *pr*

Envy Hair Studio

511 Washington Street SE at 5th Avenue E
705.3111
Open: Tu-Sa by appointment

A stylish small salon is something of a treasure in this city of hip dressers, farmers and friendly folk. I never feel like there is one trend, or one look that is the mainstay, so it is perfect to have hair stylists be as flexible as your fashion whims. Go for a new color, or a new do and you'll be amazed at what can be done at Envy without extreme cutting. *pr*

Wagner's European Bakery

1013 Capitol Way S
357.7268
Open: M-F 7a-6p, Sa 7:30a-5p
$ Veg Fr Fam

There are sweet artisan bakeries where a French sophistication imbues every gesture, order and pastry treat. Then there are the German bakeries where elbows fly, especially from the old women, in a mad rush to edge in an order for baked goods which may or may not be heard over the commotion. Wagner's goes more the route of the second scenario. Suffice to say, you may be left reeling from the whole experience. A startling spread of options includes a sandwich of chocolate between two chocolate chip cookies, marzipan horseshoe pastries with an orange glaze and baked, not fried, fritters. There are some savory food options as well from breakfast to an early dinner; afterwards you are sure crave a sugary goodie. There's also a drive-thru window if you want to skirt the over-the-counter mayhem. Auf Wiedersehen unclogged arteries! *dm*

Radiance Herbs and Massage

113 5th Avenue SE
357.9470, www.radianceherbs.com
Open: M-F 10a-7p, Sa 10a-6p, Su 12-5p

I always make sure I have someone coming to pick me up after a massage at Radiance. Because I soak in the tub for half and hour before my hour-long massage, I usually emerge with the life-energy of a wet noodle. All the massage therapists are more then qualified; all are gifted energy workers. I like to arrive early and wander through the store, which hosts a huge wall of jars containing medicinal herbs and unique teas, a natural makeup corner, and jewelry counters. With an overall emphasis on cruelty-free products, Radiance also offers their own line of natural body care products. They come in cute, reusable containers and allow you to individualize your fragrance, choosing from an all-encompassing essential oil collection. Bring back your bottles and they'll be re-used and refilled for a reduced price! *pr*

Lit Fuse
710 4th Avenue E at Cherry Street S
705.1311
Open: M-Th 12-8p F-Sa 12-10p Su 12-6p
CO

Putting a tattoo shop in the pamper section may seem a little surprising, but it would be sacrilegious not to include Lit Fuse. After all, for some people in Olympia, tattooing is a way to pamper. When I graduated from college, a friend treated me to a Lit Fuse gift certificate with owner Marco Hernandz. Adorning my feet with little hearts in honor of my accomplishment felt like the ultimate (and permanent) pamper. Established in 2000, the seasoned professionals at Lit Fuse have tons of experience and great artistic ability, so its no wonder tattoos are more then just fashion accessories to local style. Lit Fuse also has fun events like thirteen-dollar tattoo nights on Friday the thirteenth. *pr*

Fusion Integrated Body
302 Columbia Street NW
596.9696, www.fusionolympia.net
Class times vary

Rather than separating each type of healing movement into a separate business, this place, as the name says, incorporates them under one roof. After all, radiant health yoga, reiki, vibrational medicine and energy healing are interconnected with the goal of healing aches and pains, both physical and mental, in a calming way. Classes are reasonably priced and accept beginners with open arms. For more complex issues, plan a one on one session where a recipe for your body's health will be thought up using a multiplicity of techniques. *sb*

Jamie Lee and Company
309 4th Avenue E
786.6027, www.jamieleeandcompany.com
Open: Tu-Sa 10a-7p

With the ambiguous tag line, "we'll trim it, rub it or read it," Jamie Lee and her friendly staff give excellent manicures and deep conditioning treatments that cure dry hair and dead ends. While your perm is setting, you can have your astrological chart explained to you, or your Tarot cards read. Put down the gossip magazine and search your past and future while you get all pampered up. *sb*

Weekend

Fun activities for Saturdays and Sundays, plus yummy spots for brunch

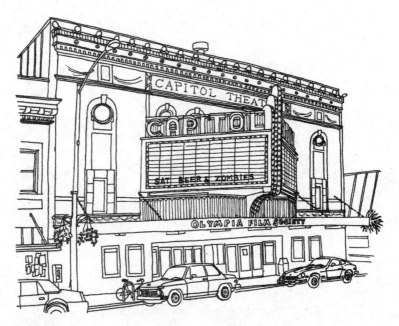

Capitol Theater

Weekends have a mood all their own. Laze around, relax with your loved ones, or explore something new. Get out of doors, or while away the hours trying out new desserts or watching bikers speed by. A short weekend getaway is a great time to see this city. Americans don't get nearly as much vacation time as allotted in some other countries, so take advantage of the weekends and kick back. *sb*

Olympia Film Society (OFS)

416 Washington Street SE # 208
754.6670, www.olyfilm.org
Show times vary

Forget about the Cineplex. Really, who needs twelve screens when all the films showing suck? What I treasure most about The Olympia Film Society is that they pre-sort through all the films for us, the only decision to make is which night you have free. Offering amazing foreign films as well as the top-picks from Hollywood's mainstream, OFS also puts on great filmic events, like "All Freaking Night" (horror films, all night long, oh my!) and the "Olympia Film Festival" (check out **Calendar** chapter for more details), which features local films. Before every show a volunteer comes out to do announcements, introduce the film and raffle off some local goodies. My feet propped up on the balcony, I enjoy the good-humored cat calling that echoes around on floor seating: it's like watching a movie at home, only better. *pr*

Bigelow House Museum

918 Glass Avenue NE at Eastbay Drive NE
753.1215, www.bigelowhouse.org
Open: Sa-Su 12-4p, allow 45 minutes for a guided tour

Olympia's oldest home has been kept up just like it was upon completion in 1860. Come tour the historic spot, overlooking the East Bay inlet, smell the roses, and check out the beautiful interior décor and architectural details. Sometimes the best way to get a sense of a new town is to peek into an old house, and here's your opportunity. *sb*

Southbay Dickersons Slow and Low BBQ

601 4th Avenue N at Cherry Street S
943.6900
Open: M-Sa 11a-9p
$ WiFi Fam Dg

Each barbecue restaurant has its own flair, and its own specialty. Southbay has managed to blend the roadhouse appeal with a put-together vibe so it feels grown up, yet still flirting with childhood. As I chow on their best dish, the pulled pork sandwich, I imagine the restaurant on the whole to be like a mid-life crisis miraculously gone right. The middle road is not an easy path to tread without getting lost in the beige and banal, but Southbay maintains a veritable down home smoke pit appeal without exuding that same rustic ambiance. I choose baked beans and potato salad instead of what most of the workers tout as the best macaroni and cheese—see where your taste buds guide you 'cause two sides come with every order, even the sandwich. They'll even deliver their finger lickin' barbecue to your door if you are located in relatively close vicinity. *sb/pr*

Boston Harbor Marina

312 73rd Avenue NE
357.5670, www.bostonharbormarina.com
Weekend Brunch starts at 8a

On weekends, the best spot for a casual family breakfast of chowder, biscuits, waffles and crumble cake is on the shaded pier at Boston Harbor. Sit on wood benches and munch away while you watch kayakers slide along the water. After eating, head down the dock to the far end where it veers right. Just at the bend, look down into the water and you'll see a hedge of white and brilliant orange anemones. Poke the pipe worms that attach themselves to the rim of the dock and their maroon brush-like tentacles will retract into their tubes. The starfish that cling to the dock poles are helping boaters by eating up pesky barnacles. Look for the deep red ones, they've traveled to Boston Harbor for a meal too, only they've come from far out in the deep sea. *sb*

Pints and Quarts Pub
1230 College Street SE, Lacey
438.9183
Bloody Mary Bar: Sa-Su 8:30a-close

Along College Street in Lacey is a rather unassuming pub with 28 beers on tap and a wonderful unique feature—a make-it-yourself Bloody Mary bar. Their house mix is the best of the tomato juice concoctions, so add as much pepper, celery salt, Tabasco and Worchestershire as you wish. It's a drink buffet! *sb*

Blue Lotus Café
412 Franklin Street SE at Capitol Way S
357.3875
Open: Tu-Sa 8a-3p
$ Vn Fr

Fill your belly in the best of ways with an all-organic vegan breakfast burrito with a hefty side of rosemary potatoes. For a truly Northwestern morning meal opt for the fluffy smoked salmon omelet with local chevre, if you ask nicely. This spot is the most calm of the breakfast joints, so it is perfect for me if I've stayed up dancing to one of Oly's bands the previous night. Sometimes I can imagine no other way to rouse up than to dive into something delicious, slow-paced and healthy at Blue Lotus. *sb*

El Guanaco
415 Water Street SW
352.5759
Open: M-Th 11a-9p, F 11a-10p, Sa 12-9p
$ Veg Fr

Guanaco serves up Salvadorian food in a restaurant heavily laden with El Salvador tourist posters and Corona and soccer paraphernalia. Salsa and chips are served immediately and the chips are warm, which always makes me happy. The papusas are pretty tasty; the chicharrón outdoes the loroco con queso. There is a full drink menu and an adjoining bar with DJ's spinning on some nights. Guanaco isn't the most outstanding cuisine, but it gets the job done when the belly calls for some sizzling and filling lunch. *dm*

Bucks Culinary Exotica Fifth Avenue
209 5th Avenue SE at Washington Street S
352.9301 www.culinaryexotica.com
Open: Tu-F 11a-5:15p, Sa 10a-4p

Buck's is a treasure-trove for cooks and kitchen geeks, they have hard to find utensils, like coconut shredders, and cute stackable spice jars. The walls are lined with jars of spices, vanilla beans, and truffles. A trip here makes me want to delve into a new recipe, or a new hobby, like being a salt epicurean. Maybe another day, today I'll buy a few new spices, at wholesale prices with no minimum amount. For the saucy side in all of us, there is Buck's, the spice place in Olympia. If you are on the bandwagon of the gourmet pepper and salt craze, you'll find black smoked salts, fleur de sel and all their fancy friends at incredibly reasonable prices in this scent-heavy store. I love the piles of jars lining all manner of shelves, all full of colorful ways to invigorate your food and your senses. Take a seat at the center table and chat it up with the shop owner about your latest culinary adventure and you'll be full of new inspirations for a weekend feast everyone will love. Dutsi the research poodle always comes with, he's positively crazy over the homemade doggy biscuits handed out here for any furry friend you bring along. *sb*

Eastside Big Tom's Burger
2023 4th Avenue E off of State Street
357.4852
Open: M-Sa 11a-8p, Su 11a-630p

Some days you need a hamburger. And some days you *need* a hamburger. Eastside Big Toms is a drive-thru burger barn famous for the special goopy-blend they slather on burgers. They still use real bananas, chocolate and peanut butter in their milkshakes, I recommend combining the three. Once you have received your brown bag of treasure with the grease spots already showing through like little beacons of light, head up the street to Lions Park (look in the **Hang Out** chapter) for a digestively fabulous walk. *pr*

Volunteer

Fun, quick, and easy ways to give back to the city

Volunteering is the best way to meet locals. Unite in a common cause to make a positive impact in some area or another, and you're sure to make fast friends. Olympians are eager volunteers, so it follows that there are some interesting opportunities for helpers. Roll up your sleeves! *sb*

Egyhop
570.0608
Roving positions
Evening and weekend short-term activities

This dedicated group of volunteers cart food, clothes and some basic hygiene and first aid items to those in need. Call ahead to meet up with a crew-member and secure a hitch of these items to your bike, or use one of theirs. Everyday or so there's a new map with deliveries that need to be made. *sb*

Olympia Food Co-Op
3111 Pacific Avenue SE (one of two locations)
956.3870
Day-long activities

Before becoming a full-time GrassRoutes groupie, I held jobs that took me behind the scenes of the everyday—teaching, stocking shelves, EMT ski patrol... you get the jist. It was so much fun to go to places where I had the inside edge. I knew what employees had to go through to make the store operate, to keep the kids in line, and to keep people safe and healthy on the slopes. At Oly Co-Op you can donate a day of your time and they'll take you behind their scenes. Each season they need support with inventory, which means you get to snack with locals all day while making Olympia's best grocer work better. Count up items while conversing on world issues. Call ahead to check current opportunities. *sb*

Wolf Haven International
3111 Offut Lake Road
264.4695 x222, www.wolfhaven.org
Day-long and long term activities

Near Olympia, in the rural town of Tenino, there's an amazing wolf preserve dedicated to the health and longevity of this magical species. Take part in their day-to-day efforts by volunteering, but don't worry they won't throw you to the wolves! Clerical work, leading tours and educational events are some of the jobs. Your help is always appreciated. Call ahead to meet one of the volunteer coordinators. *sb*

Bigelow House Museum
918 Glass Avenue NE
753.1215, www.bigelowhouse.org
Day-long activity

On Saturdays, join locals and gardening enthusiasts to help keep up the lavish beds around Olympia's oldest house. Get involved with minor fixer-upper projects, and weeding and planting. Any excuse to get mud under you nails, right? *sb*

Thurston County Animal Shelter
3120 Martin Way E
352.2510, www.jointanimalservices.org
Day-long activities

Looking out for the furry friends among us, the Thurston County Animal Shelter provides adoption services for unwanted pets, pet licensing, responsible owner education and much more. Volunteers are always needed and mostly work with the cats and dogs in adoptions. *dm*

NO IVY!
753.8380, www.ci.olympia.wa.us
Saturdays in September

English ivy is an invasive species that threatens native plants. The City of Olympia hosts work parties for volunteers to help reduce the impact of the ivy by pulling it off of native trees. Contact the City for details about how you can help. *dm*

Nisqually Reach Nature Center
4949 D'Milluhr Drive NE
459.0387, www.nisquallyestuary.org
Short and long term activities

The Puget Sound has maintained its environmental health and pristine beauty in large part from a collection of concerned groups like NRNC. By not only maintaining the estuary, but also educating residents and visitors about native wildlife, they can help ensure the future abundance of this natural environment. Volunteers can maintain aquariums, landscape, assist in the visitor center, and counsel at summer camps and educational programs. For 25 years this place has been run by dedicated volunteers, so join in the caring community. *sb*

Thurston Conservation District
www.thurstoncd.com
Various locations
Activities range from yearly commitments to day-long projects

Help deliver classroom supplies to teachers looking to educate their kids on the importance of going green. Spend a day organizing for the Green Congress. Stand behind a booth and pass out info on the local environment and the easy ways residents can curb their negative impact. There are more possibilities for much-needed volunteers at the Conservation District than perhaps anywhere else in the area. It is easy and fun to be a part of making the world a better place—what this dedicated organization spends every hour of every day doing. *sb*

MudUp
www.mudup.org
Mostly day-long activities

Join in the effort to keep Puget Sound clean and environmentally sound by checking out the MudUp website for current volunteering opportunities. Work in the mud with a good 'ol pair of Wellies, or get less muddy by working with a crew in an aquarium. There are projects all around the Sound, so check it out and find one that works with your location and time frame. You'll be grouped with other like-minded citizens, so cool conversations are sure to keep the work fun! *sb*

Olympia Film Society

754.3635, www.olyfilm.org

Olympia Film Society is simply a society of volunteers who serve freshly popped popcorn, clean the lobby, organize film festivals and project the films! They promise they can find something for just about anyone, so if you have any inclination toward free-movie tickets, allow them to show you how you can help. pr

GRuB

711 State Avenue NE
753.5522, www.goodgrub.org

GRuB stands for Garden-Raised Bounty, and they combine the eagerness and strength of their young volunteers with the need for sustainable agriculture to help low-income families feed themselves by building gardens at their homes. They have weekly drop-in hours and invite volunteers to come play in the soil, especially during the September harvests. Another good way to help GRuB is to buy from their market stand on the Westside of Olympia on the corner of Division and Elliott Streets. *pr*

Stream Team

929 Lakeridge Drive SW
754.3355 x 6377
Day or weekend-long activities

The intrepid Stream Team assumes the charge of safeguarding the watersheds of the area. Members perform plantings of native trees and shrubs to absorb runoff, post warning signs and participate in a number of other activities to keep the water clean. Contact them for the next planting project. *dm*

Bread and Roses Advocacy Center

1009 4th Avenue E
754.4588, www.breadandrosesoly.org
Some short term, mostly long-term activities

Bread and Roses is a center concerned with the creation of community to minimize class divides and serve the homeless of the area. There are also two shelters to provide housing for those who are chronically homeless. Help out with day-to-day tasks. *dm*

Free Geek Olympia
115 Olympia Avenue
705.9999, www.oly-wa.us/freegeek/
Short and long-term activities

Technology moves quickly these days and that incredibly advanced computer you just bought seems to turn obsolete after only a couple of years. With turnover such as this, a great deal of technology waste results. Free Geek recycles, reuses and restores tech gear headed for the dumps and volunteers can help test equipment, receive donations and even learn how to build a computer that they get to keep at the end of it all. *dm*

The Gleaners Coalition
402 Washington Street NE
705.0193, www.gleanerscoalition.org
Day-long activities

The Gleaners Coalition distributes fresh produce from local farms to area food banks in an effort to help alleviate hunger. Volunteers can help aid in the distribution process, tend to the growing produce and gather the fruits and vegetables from farms and gardens. *dm*

Native Plant Salvage Foundation
2918 Ferguson Street SW Suite A, Tumwater
754.3588, www.oly-wa.us/NPS/index.php
Day and week-long activities

Humans can really do quite a job of rearranging the environment, huh? Sometimes this exterior designing that we are so fond of can harm the natural order of things profoundly. This foundation advocates for the plants that were here first and are threatened by development projects. Volunteers can help in the process of relocating these plants. *dm*

Lodge

Every place to rest your noggin

If you don't have a friend to stay with in Olympia, there are a number of places where you can lay your head. Rooms in eccentrically renovated buildings, sweet B&B accommodations are exciting, but pricier options. For the low-budget traveler, motels, hostels, and camping opportunities will fit your needs. Pick a place to stay that is situated in an appealing area where you can dig in your heels and also walk to enticing destinations, so as to cut down on travel time and hit the streets of the city with the locals. *sb*

Featured Stays

Fertile Ground Guesthouse
311 9th Avenue SE
352.2428 www.fertileground.org
Two-night minimum May-September

Fertile Ground is a living, breathing model of sustainable business and living. Nestled into a luscious vegetable garden, complete with solar-powered chicken coup, the Guesthouse offers "Green Lodging for people who care." In the morning enjoy a high quality organic breakfast, served with Batdorf & Bronson's locally roasted coffee. Located downtown across from Timberland Regional Library, Fertile Ground is a great jumping off place to explore the city, or stay in for the day to enjoy their sauna, library, and one of their workshops. *pr*

Chez Cascadia
323 Milroy Street NW
570.0823 www.chezcascadia.org
Open: 9-11a or 4:30-11p

Olympia's only hostel is run by a group of inspirational twenty-somethings who created Chez Cascadia out of their own love of travel. Set in a colorful Westside house, Chez Cascadia offers both private and dorm style rooms, plus camping in the back yard. Very affordable, near major bus lines, near the Westside co-op and other fun businesses, Chez Cascadia gets my vote as the best way to get a true taste of life in Olympia. *pr*

Mid to High Range Lodging

Red Lion Hotel
2300 Evergreen Park Drive SW
943.4000

Harbinger Inn B&B
1136 East Bay Drive NE
754.0389

Swantown Inn
1431 11th Avenue SE
753.9123
www.swantowninn.com

Puget View Guest House
7924 61st Avenue NE
413.9474

Low Cost Shelter

Phoenix Inn Suites
415 Capitol Way N
570.0555

Ameritel Inn
4520 Martin Way E
459.8866

Econo Lodge
1211 Quince Street SE
943.4710

Clarion Olympia Hotel
900 Capitol Way S
367.7771

Golden Gavel Motor Hotel
909 Capitol Way S
352.8533

Olympia Inn
909 Capitol Way S
352.8533

Camping

Millersylvania State Park Camping
12245 Tilley Road S
753.1519

Salmon Shores Resort
5446 Black Lake Boulevard SW

Olympia Campground
1441 83rd Avenue SW

Nearby

Highlights from around the area

Mt. Rainier

Olympia is just one of the cities and towns lining beautiful Puget Sound. This capital city is also the gateway to the rest of the Olympic Peninsula, where wildlife abounds and tress and moss create a lush rainforest ecosystem. Take a chance to explore the towns nearby, and the natural wonders in the vicinity. Seattle isn't quite "near" enough to warrant inclusion in this book, but it has a book to itself! Take the time to explore outside the city limits—you won't be let down. *sb*

Ranch House BBQ

10841 Kennedy Creek Road SW
866.8704, www.ranchhousebbq.net
Open: Everyday 11a-9p

When we walked into Ranch House BBQ at 8:30p on a Friday night, owner and cook Amy Anderson was loudly demanding that someone get this man a bib!" We got our own personal attention from the delirious Amy, who had been at the Ranch House for 72 hours straight overseeing her award-winning slow & low BBQ that day. The $20 sampler plate showcases all the barbecue: ribblettes, chicken, hot-link sausage, pulled pork and brisket, with two sides plus cornbread. To balance the barbecue, have someone at the table order the pork loin, which is cooked tender with sage and rosemary, a classic flavor. After you are stuffed, stay for a pint of beer or a glass of cider and digest in the white and red plaid comfort of good 'ol Ranch House. *pr*

Chehalis Browser's Books

548 Market Boulevard N, Chehalis
748.4992
Open: M-Sun 10a-6p

Don't let your old books go to waste. Come to Browser's in the little town of Chehalis and trade them for some new-to-you volumes. Mostly paperbacks, the well-read ambiance of this store makes you want to take off the whole week just to read new stories and re-read your favorites. I always check their section of plays first—I seem to find just what I am looking for, even if I don't know it yet. Ask for help or just go straight to Ionesco or Eve Ensler. Re-boot your imagination! *sb*

Northwest Trek

www.nwtrek.org
Fam

Less than an hour's drive south of town is Northwest Trek, which is something like a cross between a zoo and a wildlife preserve. Hundreds of native northwestern animals live here, many of them roaming free in vast preserved habitat areas. $13.50 buys you admission to the park, guided tours and lectures, and a seat on the tram, which guides visitors through the open, back-country habitats. You may be tempted to include a stop at Northwest Trek as part of a day-trip to Mount Rainier, but you'll probably find that it takes an entire day to see everything worth seeing here. This is an excellent way to learn more about native flora and fauna, the history of human impact on the local ecosystem, and the environmental issues we currently face. Don't miss the owls or the pettable deer. *jp*

Crystal Mountain

33914 Crystal Mountain Boulevard, Enumclaw
663.2265, www.crystalmountain.com
Open: M-F 9a-4p, Sat-Sun 830a-4p

For the best verticle around, head to powder-laiden Crystal Mountain. When I was a senior in high school, my first car trips were to this epic weave of trails, where we stayed in budget hotels, rose as early as we could and hit the bumps until the lifts stopped operating. Now I might not be able to go all day like that, but I promise to try, after all, I did vow I'd be a ski bunny until I was 80. What makes Crystal especially wonderful, aside from the 3100-foot vertical drop, are the large number of lifts, which even on the best days make crowds less rampant. Varied levels are interspersed with expert terrain, so read signs carefully, and watch for powder wealthy trees runs in between the groomed stuff. If you're experienced, don't miss the very tip top of the mountain, where you can hit some righteous chutes—just remember to stay ahead of your skis! *sb*

Hiking

Olympia is cradled between the Cascade Mountains to the east and the Olympics to the northwest, and is ideally situated for hiking and camping. A scenic drive up Hood Canal will bring you to Lake Cushman (an excellent swimming destination on hot summer days), Staircase, Lena Lake, the Duckabush River, and many other pleasant hikes. Further afield is the Hoh River and the Washington Coast, one of the only completely undeveloped stretches of coastline left in the country, and one of the only patches of temperate rain forest left in the world. To the southwest is Mount Rainier National park, a very popular and incredibly scenic hiking destination where it's still possible to get away from the crowds if you know how. In fact you should be aware that some areas can be very remote, and if you decide to attempt any ambitious hikes you should be sure you know what you're doing. Always carry the Ten Essentials and be prepared for sudden weather changes, broken ankles, and other disasters. If you're looking for easier hikes closer to town the McLane Creek Nature Trail and the Nisqually Wildlife Reserve are excellent choices. *jp*

Capitol Forest

www.capitolforest.com
Open: April to October

Located five miles outside of Olympia, the Capitol Forest is a haven for recreation enthusiasts. Over 80,000 acres of trails, logging roads, trees, and many entrances, I suggest taking Delphi Road out to Waddell Creek Road. A little further down the road is the Margaret McKinney campground where the ATV and horse and hiker trails start. Go up to the weather station at the top of Capitol Peak for a view of Mt. Rainer and if it's a clear day you can even see the coast. The roads are winding and mostly unmarked, so grab a photocopied map of the trails at Olympic Outfitters. *pr*

Mount Rainier National Park

55210 238th Avenue E, Ashford
569.2211, http://nps.gov/mora

Capturing the heart, imagination, and spirit of the region, Mount Rainier or Tahoma, as it was known to the area's original inhabitants, is a Pacific Northwest icon. The 14,410-foot volcano is the most heavily glaciated mountain in the lower 48, with its upper reaches blanketed with extensive crevasse fields and towering seracs. In sharp contrast, its lower flanks are covered by old growth forests, swollen rivers, and subalpine meadows immersed in wildflowers. While countless hoards view Rainier from the relative safety and sterility of their cars and RVs, thousands each year choose to experience the mountain via the 93-mile Wonderland Trail, which encircles Rainier. If a hike isn't enough for you, you can join the ranks of the other 11,000 people—give or take—who attempt to climb Mount Rainier each year; only half of whom are successful. From classic alpine routes like Liberty Ridge, to standard lines that ascend from the mountain's two permanent high camps—Camp Muir and Camp Schurman—Rainier is a popular destination for experienced mountaineers and novice climbers alike. Despite the huge numbers of people who journey to Mount Rainier throughout the year, the mountain's expanse can still offer isolation and an unparalleled wilderness experience. *kt*

Mt. Ellinor

Open all year
Call the Hood Canal District Office for info
765.2200
www.fs.fed.us/r6/olympic/recreation-nu/trails/MtEllinor.pdf

Starting from the upper trail head, the climb to Mt. Ellinor's peak is 1.6 miles, but there is over a thousand feet of gain, most of which seems to come at the end of the hike, just when you are ready to be there already. However, the view of Hood Canal, the Cascades, and the surrounding Olympic Range makes it worth the last push. Make sure to bring water and a snack to replenish your body as you watch the wildlife abound: the mountain goats and grouse are so tame they barely get out of the way, so watch your step. A pass is required to park, so be sure to pick up a NW Forest Pass, available at forest service offices but not at trailheads. *pr*

Wild Thyme Farm & Herb'n Wisdom
72 Mattson Road, Oakville
273.8892, www.sonic.net/~wildthyme
943.5262, www.herbnwisdom.com

Located down I-5 from Olympia, Wild Thyme Farm is 150 acres full of forests, wetlands, permaculture farming and a retreat center. Wild Thyme hosts community activities and, pending the season and status of the center, opportunites to relax and rejuvenate at the retreat center. Working with Wild Thyme is Herb'n Wisdom, dedicated to providing education about permaculture and sustainable living. They hosts events and workshops in this vein. Give the farm a call to see what is happening these days. *dm*

Mount St. Helens
Gifford Pinchot National Forest
42218 NE Yale Bridge Road, Amboy
449.7800, www.fs.fed.us/gpnf/mshnvm/

In a moment, day turned into night, and gray ash rained from the skies like a tropical monsoon. For nine-hours on a Sunday morning in 1980, the earth shook, and a mushroom-shaped column ascended thousands of feet toward the heavens. In minutes, over 1,300-feet of Mount St. Helens' once nearly symmetrical cone was lost, leaving a crater 2,000-feet deep, 1.7-miles long, and 1.3-miles wide. The lore of lost societies—like Pompeii—suddenly came rushing out of history and into our own reality. The force of the eruption and earthly fallout decimated the surrounding land for nearly 150 square miles, leaving a forest of ash-covered skeletons either blown over or left eerily frozen in their skyward reach. In the aftermath of calamity, Mount St. Helens National Volcanic Monument was established, and the earth's restorative capacity has been witness first-hand ever since. The Mount St. Helens visitor center at Silver Lake—a Washington State Park—offers a comprehensive look into the mountain's history, re-growth and recovery, and is host to more than 300,000 visitors a year. For those interested in educational diversity, The U.S. Forest Service operates the Coldwater Ridge Visitor Center and The Johnson Ridge Observatory. The more adventurous can climb to the active volcano's crater rim, topping out at 8,365-feet. Although not a technical climb, the popular Monitor Ridge Route gains 4,500-feet over steep and rugged terrain in a 5-mile scramble to the top. *Kt*

Index

Bios

Serena Bartlett

Having lived and traveled in over 20 countries, Serena has devised many philosophies for seeing the world and its myriad cultures. With a degree from Long Island University's Friend's World Program, she is passionate about social justice, environmental sustainability and community. Her first guidebook, Oakland: The Soul of the City Next Door, has pioneered a unique form of travel—dubbed urban eco-travel—that combines sustainability with a local's perspective. She currently resides in Oakland with her loving partner and their toy poodle, Dutsi Bap.

Perrin Randlette

Perrin was born and raised in Olympia, WA. She has lived and traveled to many places, but still prefers the versatility and splendor of her hometown. Her degree from Evergreen State College in Visual Arts and Media Communications has provided her with the tools necessary to explore the world as a conscientious traveler. Inspired by Alain de Botton's book, The Art of Travel, Perrin sees traveling as an extension of her art. Perrin heads south in the winter, traveling through California and Mexico documenting local art and researching urban legends.

Daniel Ling

Born and raised in Oakland, Daniel's style of freehand line drawing continues to evolve with each new GrassRoutes guide, and he is known to reinterpret his illustrations into colorful paintings on wood. Daniel studied anthropology at UC Berkeley, where he learned to see beyond the superficial by putting aside all preconceived notions. He is an archaeological illustrator and freelance graphic designer.

Diana Morgan

From Japan to Central America and back to her native United States, Diana has delved into her diverse interests wherever she has set foot. Sustainable and ethical philosophies are central to her literary, bilingual journeys. She graduated from Long Island University and Friends World College and has since been a part of several practical initiatives towards environmental longevity. She lives in Portland and volunteers with kids in her free time.

Dutsi Bap

Our cheerleader, research assistant and referee, Dutsi's morale and support are crucial to the GrassRoutes team. When he's not on the road testing out new locations, he visits local nursing homes to spread joy and fluffiness. He earned his Therapy Dog certificate and believes that the meaning of life is to eat roast chicken, run in the park and take long naps on the feet of writers.